THE ONE PERCENT SOLUTION

SOLUTION

Leadership Through Action

THE ONE PERCENT SOLUTION

Leadership Through Action

by

Bijan Afkami

Cover by Paul Haven Design

International Standard Book Number:
0-9664425-0-4
Library of Congress Catalog Card Number:
98-090353

Published in 1998 by

SYNEM Leadership Center
11776 Jollyville Road, Ste. 250
Austin, TX 78759
1-888-550-LEAD
Fax: (512) 219-0383
bijan@dbcity.com

For Chris Belden, whose courage and determination in facing insurmountable challenges is the stuff of real leadership.

Your task:
to build a better world,
said God.
I answered, How?
The world is such a large vast place,
so complicated now,
and I so small and useless am;
there's nothing I can do.
But God in all His wisdom said,
Just build a better you.

— **Unknown**

ACKNOWLEDGEMENTS

This book could not have been written without the aid and support of a great many people, first and foremost that of my family. For their unwavering support and unconditional love, I am and always will be grateful. So to Heidi, Sarah, Rod and Melody — thank you. I love you all.

Leadership 101

Getting Started on the Path to Leadership

"You gain strength, courage and confidence by every experience in which you must stop and look fear in the face; you must do the thing you think you cannot do."

— Eleanor Roosevelt

This is a book grounded in reality.

We increasingly live in a society influenced by flashy advertising, clever gimmicks and instant gratification. We want the perfect job, the perfect home, the perfect relationship — and we want them all *now*, nice and quick and easy. We're prepared to pay for it, of course, provided it's immediate, but we're rarely prepared to wait.

If only learning leadership skills could work that way. If only reading one book could somehow transform us into perfect bosses, perfect employees, perfect co-workers, perfect fathers and mothers, perfect husbands and wives, perfect sons and daughters — in short, perfect people. If only . . .

But you know and I know that it doesn't work that way. We've learned through bitter experience that anything that seems too good to be true probably is. We've learned to mistrust too-colorful promises. We know that all magic wands are hollow, that the escape-proof box has a false bottom, and that the magician *always* has something up his sleeve.

I've coached a few thousand people by now about the principles of leadership, and I know that there's no trick to being a good leader — just a big dose of common sense and a lot of hard work. Unfortunately, the old maxim is true — common sense is anything but common. And most of us have about all the hard work we want right now without looking for more. Why bother?

Would you believe me if I told you that good leaders are more self-realized, more self-actualized people? They are. That doesn't mean that they're happy all the time, or always successful, or always wise and creative and inspirational. Good leaders are still fallible, still subject to the scrapes and bruises, emotional and physical, that life tends to throw our way.

But they are also more self-confident, more flexible, more empowered people. Effective leaders are winners, not whiners. They are doers, not talkers. They aren't afraid to be challenged by life. They know how to first visualize their goals and then go out and get them, confident that they can — and that they will.

Most promotions are awarded based more on leadership skills than on technical competence. Enthusiasm,

communication skills, persistence, creativity, confidence —
these are the traits that impress superiors. Simply knowing
how to do your job isn't enough to guarantee success anymore
in our hyper-competitive business world. It's only one element
among many.

Chances are you picked up this book because of its title.
You wanted to know what the gimmick was. I'm sorry to
disappoint you — there really isn't one. There are no
shortcuts to good leadership. It's a long, frequently arduous
path, and no one can walk it for you.

But that doesn't mean you have to walk the whole length
all at once. Like all journeys you can take it one step at a
time. Remember that even a single step forward brings you
that much closer to your goal. An incremental increase, no
matter how small, is still an increase.

And that's the idea behind *The One Percent Solution*. Don't
worry if you can't make speeches like Winston Churchill or
revolutionize industry like Henry Ford. Just focus on
improving your leadership skills by little steps — even by as
little as one percent — and you'll already see a change for
the better.

Not convinced that one percent is a big deal? Consider
this: on the PGA tour a few years back, two golfers, Gallagher
and Roberts, finished first and second respectively in a
tournament. Gallagher shot an average of 67.25; Roberts shot
an average of 68.25. There was only slightly more than a
one percent difference in their scores. Roberts collected
$38,225 in award money. Since Gallagher was about one

percent better, we could logically expect him to collect a one percent higher award, right? But did he? Not on your life — Gallagher collected a whopping $198,000.

There's usually no more than a one percent difference between a gold medalist's time and fourth place — but who remembers who came in fourth? Granted, these results are usually more dramatic in the world of sports than in the world of business, but the concept is sound. Even one percent can make a difference, and sometimes it makes a huge difference.

The sad reality is that we're all surrounded with so much mediocrity that even an improvement by as little as one percent can give you the competitive edge. And achieving a one percent improvement is a heck of a lot easier than trying to be Bill Gates.

Not that you should stop with one percent. Change is cumulative. By continuing to improve little by little you'll find that, in time, you've actually improved by a considerable margin.

Cathy F. had had about as tough a life as you can imagine. Her parents divorced when she was five. She lived with her mother, who was an alcoholic. Her brother ran away from home when she was nine and she never saw him again. Cathy was in constant trouble at school, and by the time she was a teenager she was a drug addict. She quit school at 16, left home and bounced from town to town, stealing to support her habit. When she was 20 she was arrested and convicted of theft and fraud and sentenced to five years in prison.

LEADERSHIP 101

I met her in her fourth year there. I was conducting life skills/leadership seminars for a select group of inmates, and she applied and was accepted into the program. Despite some initial reservations, she made a sincere commitment to participate with an open and enthusiastic mind.

At the course's end I asked her what, if anything, she had learned from it. She told me, "I've learned that leadership is a way of life. It's about how I approach challenge."

By learning how to focus on small, attainable improvements Cathy acquired the momentum she needed to move towards her goals. She became a more confident, happy, determined person, a real leader to her fellow inmates. Once released, she pursued a newly-discovered talent — art. These days, she frequently returns to prison to help counsel others — and she recently sold some of her work to a prestigious New York gallery. One percent made a tremendous difference in Cathy's life.

Your situation doesn't have to be as desperate or dramatic as Cathy's to still profit from the one percent idea. A former student of mine, Jaime Idunate, a Manufacturing Supervisor at Motorola, wrote me about the changes he's made in his life since the seminar. "I have developed an enormous amount of self-confidence and motivation to succeed in all areas of my life," he wrote. "I've received two promotions and have been honored with one of my company's most distinguished awards based on my performance. The enthusiasm and drive . . . has also spilled over into my family life, where I feel confident about the future as a new father and husband."

BALANCING THE WHEEL OF LIFE

I believe one percent can make a tremendous difference in your life too if you're willing to give it a chance. But remember: leadership isn't just about managing people. It concerns how we lead all aspects of our lives — how we work with our co-workers, how we show love to our friends and families, how we make our community a better place. For good leaders, the wheel of life is in harmony — no single spoke dominates, throwing it off track. There is instead a balance between career, education, spiritual well-being, finances, physical fitness, family and friends, personal relationships and community service.

An old Japanese proverb says that "Wisdom and virtue are like the two wheels of a cart." Unless both are in place operating together, the cart cannot move forward. I'd like to amend that to read "Leadership in our professional lives and leadership in our personal lives are like the two wheels of a cart." Not as catchy, perhaps, but more illustrative of what I'm trying to get across. Don't neglect one for the other, or you won't be able to move forward as a leader, either. Leadership affects *all* aspects of our lives, remember.

The subtitle of this book is "Leadership Through Action." Since we've just talked a little about leadership itself, I think now is a good time to emphasize the action part of the formula. Unless you take action, unless you apply what you learn in the following pages, you can't become a fully-realized leader. Theory isn't enough. Knowing what you *should* do isn't enough. To succeed, you've got to get out there and do it.

We all have a mental picture of "the perfect me." And we all know that there is usually a sizable gap between that image and reality. But if we sense as we move through life that the gap is narrowing, that we're getting closer to our ideal, then our lives become richer. We're encouraged by our progress. We become more impassioned, more excited, more alive.

If, on the other hand, that gap seems to widen, we become discouraged, listless and frustrated. Our life becomes rut-laden; dull routine rules our existence. Life becomes a chore.

The only way to narrow the gap between where we are and where we would like to be is to take action. There is no substitute. To encourage you, I've included a short worksheet at the end of every chapter. Each one will help you focus on one area in which you can take definite action, using the leadership skills you've learned in the preceding chapter. Please don't ignore these exercises — they're designed to help you transform leadership theory into leadership action.

Ralph Waldo Emerson once defined success this way: "To laugh often and much; to win the respect of intelligent people and the affection of children; to earn the appreciation of honest critics and endure the betrayal of false friends; to appreciate beauty; to find the best in others; to leave the world a bit better, whether by a garden patch or a redeemed social condition; to know even one life has breathed easier because you have lived — this is to have succeeded."

Don't seek material success alone. While it is unquestionably pleasant, is also elusive — and fleeting. Believe me, I know. I came to this country from Iran in the late 70s. Within a decade I had achieved a sizable degree of monetary success. I had several business and real estate holdings, a beautiful house, a great car.

Then Austin's real estate market crashed.

Suddenly I was flat broke. I was forced to declare bankruptcy. The bank foreclosed on our home. And as my wife and I drove around looking at rental homes — in neighborhoods I never thought I'd have to live in — all I could think was, "How am I going to scrape together enough money for a security deposit?"

A few years later we had painfully struggled back to a reasonable measure of economic security. My wife and I had worked hard and it finally appeared that we'd turned the corner on our financial hardships. We had even managed once again to buy a house of our own.

One weekend we took our kids to Fiesta Texas in San Antonio — our first vacation in over a year. We had a terrific time and arrived back in Austin after dark. As we neared our home we could see some sort of commotion, and as we drove up the awful truth became apparent — our house had burned completely to the ground.

It was a terrible shock, but I was just grateful that no one was hurt. I shudder to think of what may have happened if we'd all been home. I realized that compared to the safety of my family, money was pretty meaningless. The emotional success we enjoyed as a family was indescribably more important than any material success I might have achieved as a businessman.

We rebuilt our lives again, step by step. And that taught me the value of patience, of persistence, of faith. We can't change the world all at once. We can't become perfect people in the blink of an eye. Sometimes all we can do, as Voltaire said, is to tend to our own gardens. But sometimes that's enough.

There's not a lot of academic theory in this book. It's designed to be a leadership primer, to offer practical advice and honest examples, to give you some valuable tools to put in your leadership tool box. I've used a lot of anecdotes and quotes because I think they're memorable, inspirational and succinct. If you're reading along and you suddenly exclaim,

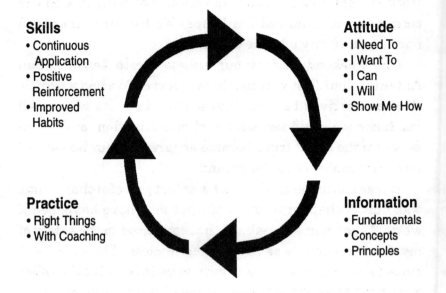

Skills
• Continuous
  Application
• Positive
  Reinforcement
• Improved
  Habits

Attitude
• I Need To
• I Want To
• I Can
• I Will
• Show Me How

Practice
• Right Things
• With Coaching

Information
• Fundamentals
• Concepts
• Principles

"But that's just common sense!" then great — I've done what I set out to do.

How to Approach This Book

Take a look at the above graphic for a demonstration of a successful learning process.

It all starts with the right attitude: saying, "I need to" or "I want to" and "I can" and "I will" and "Show me how." Then I'll try to give you the information you want, the fundamentals, the concepts, the principles involved. Your job then is to practice those things, ideally with coaching. That will produce new skills, which, with continuous application and positive reinforcement, will result in improved habits. And those habits will help foster a positive attitude, allowing you to continue the cycle.

Leadership is a never-ending journey. And, like so many things, it's the journey itself that makes us better, stronger, more confident human beings. You're about to set out on one of the most exciting quests you could ever undertake. You'll learn about hidden strengths and talents you never suspected you had, you'll learn to appreciate the richness of life in all its infinite variety, you'll learn to establish better, deeper, more lasting and more satisfying relationships with others.

Above all, you'll learn what Cathy F. did: it's never too late to change. Leadership isn't a gimmick; it's a way of life. Embrace it and the possibilities really are limitless.

CHAPTER 1

Dare to be Confident
How to Expand Your Comfort Zone

"Who dares, wins."

**— motto of England's elite
Special Air Service**

 I came to the United States from Iran in the late 70s. Although it was an excellent time to leave Iran, it was a less-than-ideal time to be an Iranian in America. Tensions between the two countries were high. The Shah was on the verge of being toppled, Iranian militants blamed the U.S. for all of Iran's problems — and then, the capstone: the hostage crisis.

Now I had left Iran precisely to get away from that sort of thing. I was no radical. I just wanted to obtain a college education and live out the American Dream, which is, when you really think about it, the dream of just about everyone around the globe.

That didn't change the fact that I was still an Iranian at a time when Iranians couldn't have been more unpopular over here. I became hypersensitive about it, despite the fact that I had made some friends and no one had tried to lynch me. It didn't matter. I was still afraid of being rebuffed, ridiculed, scorned, ignored, insulted, laughed at, yelled at or sneered at.

At parties I found myself quietly finding a nice, safe corner to hide in. I tried not to talk to anyone, to smile, to look anyone in the eye. I tried to make myself invisible. I threw up a shell of isolation and, not surprisingly, it worked. I was left alone. I was also miserable.

I thought that my actions were shielding me from harm, but I finally realized that what was really happening was that my self-confidence was being further eroded. My comfort zone — the range of situations in which I felt most confident — was gradually shrinking thanks to all that negative reinforcement.

So I made a conscious decision to expand my comfort zone. Instead of skulking in corners, I determined that I would actively seek out conversation. I would walk up to people, introduce myself and see what happened. I wouldn't play the wallflower any longer.

It wasn't easy making the transition. I was intensely nervous the first few times I approached a group of people I didn't know. Things didn't always go as well as I would have wished — but no one threw rocks at me, either. And I found that the more I did it, the easier it became. The more relaxed

DARE TO BE CONFIDENT

I was, the more successful I was.

Now I make it a point at parties to find those poor, shy, obviously uncomfortable individuals hiding in corners and try to draw them out of their self-imposed shells.

The idea of comfort zones is a fairly straightforward one. We all know the activities in which we excel, the people we're comfortable talking to, the places we like to go, the topics we're knowledgeable about. All these things compose the tapestry of our daily lives.

New people, strange situations, foreign activities, other places — because we're not used to any of these, they tend to make us nervous, anxious and uncomfortable. We have an instinctive tendency to stick with what's familiar — with what's safe. And it's those familiar people, places and activities that compose our comfort zone. It's within that sphere of activity that we're most relaxed, most happy, most confident and most productive.

It's completely natural to stay with the tried and true. Conservatism isn't necessarily a bad thing. But it can be carried to an unhealthy extreme. Medieval Spaniards, for instance, were so repulsed by the idea of change that they took their leave of each other by saying, "May no new thing arise." If we avoid any and all change, if we choose only to dig our rut ever deeper, then we also avoid the possibility of growth — personal growth, spiritual growth, economic growth, professional growth.

Growth is sometimes painful, awkward and embarrassing (remember your teenage years), but it also enriches our lives.

THE ONE PERCENT SOLUTION

It allows us to discover new talents, to improve existing skills, to learn more about the world around us. Growth makes us more complete individuals. Change may not always be positive, but growth surely is.

The problem is that growth requires us to push the boundaries of our comfort zones. It means taking chances and making mistakes. It means bruising our egos and possibly our bodies. It isn't easy. It isn't always fun. It definitely is *not* comfortable.

But it is necessary if we hope to become fully-realized human beings and effective leaders. Narrow comfort zones are nothing but emotional prison cells. They're cages. Comfortable cages, perhaps, but a gilded cage is still a cage, remember. We have to make a conscious commitment to breaking out of those cages. We have to seek out new experiences, new situations, new activities.

And if we can weather the initial discomfort they bring, we'll soon discover something wonderful: the more we expose ourselves to these new things, the more comfortable we'll be doing them. Before we realize it, we've incorporated them into our comfort zone — or, rather, it's grown to encompass them.

Why do leaders need an ever-broadening comfort zone? Simple. Leaders are called upon to deal with all sorts of people and all sorts of situations. Leaders have to expect the unexpected. They have to be creative, adaptable, flexible, cool under pressure and calm in a crisis. They have to have the confidence that they can handle any new situation, and, given time, master it.

Narrow comfort zones prevent us from taking advantage of windows of opportunity as they present themselves. Broad comfort zones give us the self-confidence necessary to take risks, to try new things, to grasp goals at the utmost edge of our reach. Remember this: *Self-confidence is the foundation of all worthwhile achievement.*

In his essay, "The Common Denominator of Success," Albert E. Gray wrote, "All successful people have the habit of doing things failures don't like to do. They don't like to do them either, necessarily, but their dislike is subordinated to the strength of their purpose."

You can't become self-confident by snapping your fingers. It's not a magic trick. It takes hard work and perseverance, and you have to prepare yourself for setbacks. But you can't be discouraged by them. Above all else, realize this: it's going to take time.

And sometimes taking a little time is all it takes. Dr. M. Scott Peck is the author of the bestselling *The Road Less Traveled* and several other books. He told a story once that illustrates how even seemingly successful people can be self-conscious about their shortcomings.

Although Dr. Peck was an amazingly successful psychiatrist and author, he said he always considered himself a mechanical idiot. He simply couldn't fix things — even simple, everyday things. A broken doorbell had him staring helplessly. A nonfunctional toaster had him running for help.

While taking a walk one day he saw his neighbor repairing

a lawn mower. Dr. Peck said hello, and then remarked, "You know, I really admire you. I've never been able to fix things."

"That's because you don't really take the time," the neighbor said.

A few days later, the parking brake became stuck on a patient's car. The lady told Dr. Peck that she knew *something* under the dashboard could release the stubborn brake, but she didn't know what exactly it was, or where exactly it was.

Dr. Peck's first impulse was to let her call AAA, but he remembered his neighbor's words and felt challenged to see if he could fix the problem, provided he actually took the time to try. Pushing aside his doubts and feelings of inferiority, he lay on the floor of the car and studied the wires and switches he found. Without feeling rushed, he read the labels and followed the paths of the pertinent wires.

Finally, after several minutes, he found the right switch. A single motion unfroze the brake. Dr. Peck said he realized then that he wasn't defective in solving mechanical problems — provided he took the time and gave it his best effort.

Dr. Peck's example also demonstrates the importance of gathering as much knowledge about a subject as we can before undertaking a new action. We all know that knowledge is power. Power breeds confidence. That means that, in effect, knowledge produces confidence.

Franklin Roosevelt was once asked about making decisions as President. He said, "I study my subject, and I have personal confidence in my decision." His confidence was due in large part to that very process of study and information gathering.

It's impossible to under-emphasize that point. Good leaders study, study, study. They learn, learn, learn. Whether it's through seminars, books, formal classes or simply listening to the experience and expertise of others, effective leaders know about the value of prior preparation. Knowledge *is* power.

Self-respect is another crucial ingredient in building self-confidence. Too often we castigate ourselves for past failures — even those that weren't our fault. It's one thing to examine past mistakes to learn from them. It's quite another to dwell on them exclusively. We're all human. We're all fallible. We have to accept that and learn to forgive ourselves — and move on.

Steve was an up-and-coming young executive who seemed to be on the fast track. He had a great office view, a commanding salary and great stock options. On the flip side, however, his job was filled with enough pressure to make him pop aspirin as though they were breath mints. Steve knew that one bad decision, one lost account, one poor presentation and he could end up sorting packages in the mail room.

Steve could feel the pressure mounting, and he knew it was starting to get to him. So he made arrangements to visit an elderly uncle, a man who had always been an inspiration to him.

The wise old man had suffered a stroke a few years previously, and Steve found that he and his wife had retired to a small farm in Missouri. He greeted Steve warmly upon his arrival and, sensing Steve's distress, asked him about his problem. Steve poured out all his job-related fears and anxieties.

The old man listened quietly. After Steve finished, he paused a moment and then said, "Your problem is that you're grief-stricken."

"But no one's died!" Steve said. "I haven't lost anyone."

"You've lost your confidence," Steve's uncle said. "That's why you're grief-stricken. You've got to go through the stages of mourning your loss — and then get busy rebuilding your self-image."

Steve's uncle motioned him over to a window. He pointed out the maple trees planted at the edge of the property. The former owner had sought to avoid the hard work of digging postholes for a fence, and instead had simply strung barbed wire from tree to tree. Steve's uncle asked him to notice how some of the trees were unscarred by the wire while others had become misshapen and bent.

"Life's routines are the same with people," he said. "Some events act just as they were conceived; others cause bending. Each individual must adjust to both types. Some people have injuries and others remain unhurt. To remain straight a person must learn not to bear grudges — not even towards himself. People must forgive themselves and others, and then start rebuilding their self-confidence and planning new goals."

If life throws obstacles in our path that make us stumble

and fall, we've got to accept the fact that we fell down — and then we've got to get right back up and continue on our way.

Marjorie Holmes said, "People build self-respect by their willingness to accept help when needed and by rising after a failure. Self-confidence will grow as continuing effort brings success. Remember that it is possible that the largest lump of self-respect may come from realizing that failure in some project made room for success that was twice as important to your career. Don't forget that self-confidence grows when used. People must dare to try the difficult task."

And failure isn't foreordained. Sometimes those obstacles, instead of causing us to stumble, cause us to leap ahead. "Struggling against obstacles makes an individual stronger," writes David Marain. "Sometimes a leader must conquer a problem because so much is expected of him."

The key is taking action. It's not always easy. It requires effort, and usually we'd much rather just sit back and let someone else do something. It's a natural law, really — homeostasis, the tendency of objects to remain in the same state or condition until acted upon by an outside force. Literally, it means "to remain dormant, to stand in the same place."

But the wonderful thing about being human beings is that we possess the gift of rational thought. We're not just prisoners of our instincts and emotions. We can recognize that homeostasis is a natural tendency — but it's a tendency, not an imperative. We *can* change, provided we're willing to fight our instinctive inertia. We can break out of those narrow cages that confine our lives.

How to Achieve a Breakthrough in Your Life

1. Make a commitment. Football coach Lou Holtz once joked about the difference between being merely involved and being truly committed to a cause: "I had bacon and eggs for breakfast today. The chicken was involved but the pork was committed."

The greatest experiences in life arise from true commitment. Your best days are not those of leisure, but those devoted to a cause. They may be days of struggle, of effort, of hard labor. But they will also be the days worth remembering.

2. Visualize yourself doing it. In his book, *The New Dynamics of Winning*, Dennis Waitley writes, "Champions see the act of winning in advance. They know that 'what you see is who you'll be.' A champion will focus all of his or her thoughts and energy on the goal and move towards it. If you can see yourself as a champion in your mind's eye and you imagine it over and over again, you will begin to believe it is really true. As a result, your attitude and your action, both physical and mental, will move to bring about the reality of the image you are visualizing."

When my children were younger, they decided that what

the family really needed was a dog. We already had two birds and a cat, so my wife and I weren't anxious to add another pet. But the kids wouldn't give up — especially my daughter Melody, who kept getting us to visualize the dog she wanted. She talked about how small and white and fluffy it was. Sometimes she'd act like she was playing with an imaginary dog.

Well, eventually I let myself get talked into going to the Humane Society — just to look, mind you. But once there we saw a little toy poodle that so perfectly matched the visual image Melody had put into our minds that we felt obliged to play with it. And that pretty much sealed the deal; Monique the poodle became a beloved member of the family — thanks in no small part to Melody's ability to visualize her goal.

3. Take risks. It's risky to just jump right in — there's no glossing over that. But we shouldn't let ourselves be afraid of risk. As good leaders, risk is our business. I've incorporated a wonderful passage about the value of risk into my leadership seminars. I've had it so long I don't know who originally wrote it — I don't know if anyone knows anymore — but I think it's both inspiration and comforting:

To laugh is to risk appearing the fool.
To weep is to risk appearing the sentimental.
To reach out to another is to risk involvement.
To expose feeling is to risk exposing your true self.
To place your ideas, your dreams before the crowd is to

risk their loss.
To love is to risk not being loved in return.
To live is to risk dying.
To hope is to risk despair.
To try is to risk failure.
But risk must be taken, because the greatest hazard in
life is to risk nothing!
The person who risks nothing, does nothing, has
nothing, and is nothing.
He may avoid suffering and sorrow, but he simply
cannot learn, feel, change, grow, love and live.
Chained by his certitude, he is a slave.
He has forfeited freedom.
Only a person who risks . . . is free.

4. Help others. Another great way to expand our comfort zones is to make a commitment to help others. Not only do we get the joy and satisfaction of sharing our knowledge or bettering another's life, but by seeing other people's problems we frequently are better able to put our own in perspective. Suddenly they don't seem all that insurmountable after all.

Joe and Sue were a young newlywed couple. Joe had found a good job right out of college, but his self-confidence took a real blow when he didn't get a raise after his first year there. Sue, meanwhile, was having trouble adjusting to life in the big city. She was very shy and didn't make friends easily, and although she had good computer skills, didn't think she could compete for a job in such a large market.

DARE TO BE CONFIDENT

One day the couple saw a notice in their church's bulletin asking for a computer-savvy volunteer who could donate a few hours a week to working in the church office. At Joe's urging, Sue offered her services and soon found the position to be extremely enjoyable.

A few weeks later, Joe was surprised when Sue told him she wanted to take him to the YMCA for swimming lessons.

"But I already know how to swim," Joe protested. "I used to teach swimming at summer camp!"

"That's just it," said Sue. "I told the people at the church that you'd make a wonderful instructor."

"The people" were from a community youth program designed to help underprivileged kids learn to stay afloat — in more ways than one.

Once he started teaching again, Joe realized that he'd forgotten the sheer joy of helping others. With an outlet for his energies, he regained his former enthusiasm and optimism. He suddenly wasn't as consumed by his failure to win that raise. And, interestingly enough, a few months after Joe started rebuilding his self-confidence by helping others, he was offered a major job promotion.

As Emerson said, "It is one of the beautiful compensations of this life that no one can sincerely try to help another without helping himself." Sometimes, though, it happens in ways we simply don't expect.

Several years ago I was attempting to hook up a new VCR. It's not rocket science, I know, but like so many of us I have trouble setting the clock on the things, much less actually plugging all those cables into the right outlets. While I was puzzling over what to put where, my son Rod, only six years old at the time, came over to help.

My first impulse was to shoo him away — distractions were definitely *not* what I needed at the moment. But then I reconsidered. It might be good for his self-confidence to learn a little about this sort of thing.

What I hadn't realized was that my son, a product of the Nintendo generation, was far more conversant than I was in the fine art of video hookups. Rod had everything working in no time. I was amazed, and bragged to my wife about our boy's prowess. And Rod beamed from ear to ear — his self-confidence had been given a big boost by my sincere pride and admiration.

5. Just do it. Philip Knight had an idea back in the 1960s to import running shoes from Japan and sell them in the U.S. He had just $1,000 in start-up capital, and initially sold the shoes from the back of his station wagon. His former college coach, William Bowerman, joined him in 1963 and helped improve the shoes' design. Today, Nike, Inc. has a market value of over $3.5 billion.

It would've been easy for Phil Knight to hold off taking action until he raised more money, or had a storefront, or had more experienced partners. But instead he jumped right in, confident he had a good idea and that he could handle whatever problems arose. He knew he could learn on the job. He wasn't afraid to take a risk — and look how it paid off.

The original leadership guru, Dale Carnegie, used to tell a story (originally written by Elbert Hubbard) entitled "A Message to Garcia." The characters involved are a little dated, perhaps, for modern readers, but the moral is timeless.

About a century ago, when war broke out between Spain and the United States, Cuba was very much a focal point of hostilities. It was an unhappy Spanish colony at the time, and insurrection had broken out some time before. The American high command decided to immediately contact Garcia, the leader of the rebellion, in order to secure his cooperation against the Spanish troops on the island.

There was a problem, though: no one knew exactly where Garcia was. Somewhere in the mountains, hiding from the Spanish — that much was known. But where exactly? Who knew? Beyond the reach of mail or telegram, that much was certain.

Someone told President McKinley that if anyone could find Garcia and deliver the message, it was a man named Rowan. So the President sent for him, explained the importance of the task, and handed him the letter. Rowan took the letter without comment, put it into a waterproof oilskin pouch, placed it inside his shirt, and left.

Four nights later he was covertly landed on the Cuban coast by open boat. He entered the jungle on foot and for three weeks scoured the hostile countryside until at last he found Garcia on the other side of the island and delivered the message.

THE ONE PERCENT SOLUTION

And while his determination and courage are certainly praiseworthy, what impressed Carnegie most was simply this: when given the letter, Rowan didn't ask, "Where is he?" He didn't point out the difficulties involved, or ask how he was to go about finding Garcia, or who would help him, or whether there wasn't a better way. No — he took the letter and just did it.

Making a personal breakthrough won't necessarily come easily. It means taking chances, making mistakes, enduring criticism. But experienced leaders know that criticism comes with the job. You can't make all of the people happy all of the time. There's always someone who claims he could've done a better job, or that you shouldn't have done this or done that, or that you definitely should have done that. So what?

If the suggestions are valid, make the necessary corrections so that the same mistakes don't occur in the future. But if it's just petty or sniping or nitpicking, then let it roll of your back like water off the proverbial duck. It's not worth compromising your sense of self-worth.

When Abraham Lincoln was running for President, some of his opponents circulated a slanderous story that he had a secret mistress and was living an adulterous life. So what did this great man do to dam the rising tide of rumor? Nothing! He said that in this instance any defense he could offer was probably useless — his friends didn't need an explanation, and his enemies wouldn't believe any he gave.

Constructive feedback is worth listening to and

considering; destructive criticism is not.

Sometimes that's easier said than done, of course. No matter how much we want to remain aloof, we can't help but be affected by the way others see us. Man is a social animal — we crave the acceptance of others.

I remember a time when my kids decided to give our poodle Monique a haircut — a mohawk, to be precise. The poor dog looked really awful. We had a party that evening, and as our guests came in and saw the badly-shorn pup, they all had a good laugh. You wouldn't expect that to bother a dog, but for the next few days Monique, normally an affectionate and outgoing animal, seemed shy and withdrawn. I honestly think she was embarrassed by her haircut. Maybe humans aren't the only creatures sensitive to ridicule.

Here's a final few thoughts I'd like to leave you, from Nelson Mandela's 1994 inaugural address. I hope these words will help inspire you to seek out new experiences, to risk deeply, to journey down the road not taken:

"Our deepest fear is not that we are inadequate. Our deepest fear is that we are powerful beyond measure. It is our light, not our darkness, that most frightens us. We ask ourselves, 'Who am I to be brilliant, gorgeous, talented and fabulous?'

"Actually, who are you not to be? You are a child of God. Your playing small doesn't serve the world. There is nothing enlightened about shrinking so that other people won't feel insecure around you. We were born to make manifest the glory of God that is within us. It's not just in some of us; it's in everyone. And as we let our own light shine, we unconsciously give other people permission to do the same. As we are liberated from our fear, our presence automatically liberates others."

Conclusion

We all have comfort zones — spheres of activity in which we're confident and experienced. Effective leaders know that growth can only be achieved by expanding the boundaries of those comfort zones. It isn't always easy. It involves risk and change and the chance of failure. But the more we expose ourselves to new situations, new activities and new people, the more flexible and self-confident we will become.

Self-confidence isn't a tangible goal we can grab. It's an ongoing journey. It requires a continuing commitment, an open mind and a thick skin. Sometimes the best way to expand our horizons is by helping others. Above all, we must take action. We shouldn't fear risk — nothing worthwhile was ever achieved without it.

CH. 1 PERSONAL WORKSHEET

"Make the most of yourself,
for that is all there is of you."

— Ralph Waldo Emerson

I will expand my comfort zone by at least 1% by experiencing this one new thing:

_____

_____

_____

_____

I will benefit by this 1% improvement in the following way:

_____

_____

_____

_____

CHAPTER 2

Attitude is Key
The Continuing Power of Positive Thinking

*"Nothing great was ever achieved
without enthusiasm."*

— Ralph Waldo Emerson

One blisteringly hot summer day, a group of railroad workers were repairing a stretch of track in the railway depot of one of the major lines. They finished with one gap and were trudging their way to the next when, on an adjacent track, a locomotive with a number of ornate private cars rolled into the station. One of the workers, Ray, a grizzled older man who'd been with the railroad for at least 30 years, pointed towards the new arrival and mentioned that it was the company president's personal train.

Just then the president himself, a distinguished gentleman always impeccably dressed, stepped from the train. He glanced over to the group of workers, paused, and

43

called out, "Ray, is that you? Come on over here! It's been ages!"

The other workers watched in amazement as Ray strolled over to the president and the two chatted agreeably for several minutes. When Ray returned to his buddies, they plied him with questions about his encounter — most wanted to know why the president seemed so chummy towards him.

"Well," Ray replied, "we both started workin' here on the same day, both of us layin' track."

"So how come he's the company president and you're still layin' track?" one of the younger men asked.

"Well," Ray paused and scratched his chin. "Well, guess mebbe it's because back when we started here, I was workin' for $40 a month, but he was workin' for the company."

Attitude is often the single most important determinant of whether we succeed or fail. Successful leaders see opportunities where others see only obstacles. They rejoice in challenge, knowing that it will bring out the best in them, allow them to stretch themselves, to acquire new knowledge, to demonstrate their competence.

Those who shy away from challenge, who see only the cloud and never the silver lining, who see only half-empty glasses — how they can possibly expect to motivate others? They can't even motivate themselves.

Charles Swindall once wrote:

"The longer I live, the more I realize the impact of attitude on life. Attitude, to me . . . is more important than the past, than education, than money, than circumstances, than failures, than successes, than what other people think or say or do. It is more important than appearance, giftedness or skill. It will make or break a company, a church, a home. The remarkable thing is we have a choice every day regarding the attitude we will embrace for that day.

"We cannot change our past . . . we cannot change the fact that people will act in a certain way. We cannot change the inevitable. The only thing we can do is play on the one string we have, and that is our attitude. I am convinced that life is 10% what happens to me and 90% how I react to it. And so it is with you . . . we are in charge of our attitude."

Swindall's advice boils down to this: We don't always have as much control over *what* happens as we would like, but we have complete control over *how* we will respond. Engendering a positive outlook, both in ourselves and others, is both a proactive and a reactive process. It's during a crisis when our morale is most sorely tested — that's when we really, really need a positive, optimistic outlook. It's during those times we want to remain unruffled, cool, calm and collected.

But unless we've worked to make those traits part of our everyday life, we can't count on them magically appearing when problems strike. Developing a positive mental attitude is like developing a successful exercise regimen — you won't see results unless you stick with it. Working out once a month won't help you shape up, and remembering to be enthusiastic only once in a blue moon won't strengthen your mental resilience. You've got to be consistently positive, in both your professional and personal life.

THE ONE PERCENT SOLUTION

I know this doesn't sound easy. And it sometimes isn't, especially at first. We've all accumulated a lot of bad attitude habits over the course of our lifetime, and those don't just disappear. When faced with adversity we tend to fall into the old patterns; the challenge — *challenge*, remember, not *problem* — is to create new, more positive patterns to supersede the old.

I've found that one way to maintain my positivity is to read others' inspirational stories — I marvel at the way some of these folks overcome obstacles that make the mountains barring my way seem like anthills. It's a sure cure for feel-sorry-for-myself-itis.

Here's one of my favorite examples of the can-do, never-say-quit attitude of real leaders:

Joyce and Larry always sensed an "I'm sure I can" attitude in their son Bryan, who had muscular dystrophy. By the time the boy entered kindergarten walking was already painful for him, but Bryan wanted no help getting up whenever he fell. He wanted to do it on his own.

By the time Bryan was nine, his legs were so weak that his doctors decided to confine him to a wheelchair. They couldn't confine his spirit, though — he cheerfully told his anxious mother not to be sad. Since he couldn't stand, he'd ride instead.

Bryan accepted his inability to participate in sports, but he didn't use his disability as an excuse to withdraw into a shell of self-pity. He became an excellent student, even tutoring his friends when they fell behind. By helping others he was able to refocus attention, his own and others', away from his disease.

When it came time for his junior high graduation, Bryan surprised his mother by declaring that he wanted to attend the farewell dance. His mother, afraid he'd be hurt — emotionally, not physically — tried to talk him out of going. She gently told him, "Bryan, I don't think many girls will be confident enough to try and dance with a boy in a wheelchair."

"That's true," Bryan replied, "but it's my farewell dance, too. I'm going to go."

On the night of the dance, Joyce helped her son put on his new suit and drove him to the junior high gym. "If you get bored, call me," she said as she unloaded his wheelchair from the van. He just smiled. She cried all the way home.

At 9:45 the phone rang. "It was a great dance!" Bryan said. "I'm going to go out for pizza now with a couple of guys and their dates. They'll get me home."

Joyce's heart sang. "Just like any kid calling his mother!" she thought.

During his senior year in high school, Bryan's disease became more aggressive and he weakened rapidly. He knew how much worse he was becoming, but he continued to lead as normal a life as he could. He was determined that he'd get his diploma, no matter what. He even continued his tutoring duties.

Bryan died during the spring of his senior year. But on graduation night that June, the diploma he had worked so hard for was presented to his mother. She told a hushed and tearful crowd, "If Bryan were here he'd say, 'See, I told you I'd do it.' I say, let's not be sad. Let's remember that Bryan is no longer confined to that wheelchair. He's free of it; he's like any other kid. Let's rejoice at his success, just as he would have."

Bryan realized early that life is never perfect, and that complaining won't make it so. He accepted what he was given, made the most he could of it, and in the end exceeded nearly everyone's expectations. He didn't see himself as disabled, just challenged, and he refused to allow those challenges to impede the fullness of his life, short as it was.

It's important that every once in a while you take the time to catalogue your blessings. Take an inventory of all the good things in your life — you may be pleasantly surprised. We all spend so much time identifying problems that we too often neglect to identify life's gifts. Norman Vincent Peale once said, "A positive thinker does not refuse to recognize problems to exist; he merely refuses to dwell on them."

Here's another story that illustrates the value in making a habit of positive thinking:

Jeanne Hill and her husband had recently relocated to Arizona, and after a summer of sweltering in the desert heat, Jeanne felt like she had had enough. By the following April she was already dreading the prospect of another three months of the scorching temperatures.

She happened to mention that in passing to old Mr. Simpson at his service station in Phoenix while he was filling her car's tank. "Now, you don't want to worry the season that way," he chided her gently. "Dreadin' the scorchers just makes the summer start sooner and last longer."

Jeanne realized that Mr. Simpson was right — her anxiety transformed three months of summer into a five-month hot spell, and ruined the joys of spring in the process.

"Treat the heat like a welcome surprise," Mr. Simpson advised. "Take advantage of the best that our summers offer and ignore the rest in the air-conditioning."

"Is there a best about summer here?" she asked weakly.

"Ever been up at five or six o'clock?" he replied. "I swear, those July mornin' skies are so rosy it seems like heaven is blushin'. On August nights the stars look like icebergs floatin' in a dark blue ocean. An' a person don't know the real joy of swimmin' til he's jumped into the water on a 114-degree day!"

A young employee who'd been standing nearby grinned and said softly, "Well, you've just had Simpson's Special — free with any fill-up."

To Jeanne's amazement, Mr. Simpson's advice was sound. She was able to enjoy April and May without dread. And when the scorchers did arrive, she adjusted her schedule to accommodate the heat. She worked in the garden during the cool of the morning. In the afternoons she took naps with her children. She learned in the summers that followed to appreciate the unparalleled beauty of a desert sunrise.

When Jeanne and her family were transferred to Ohio, they used the same attitude to deal with the bitter cold and heavy snows of a northern winter. They adjusted their schedules and their recreational activities, and learned to appreciate the pristine beauty of newly-fallen snow, the exhilaration of ice-skating on a frozen pond, the cozy charm of a fire on a winter's night.

A few years later they returned again to the desert. Jeanne found Mr. Simpson in a smaller service station in a nearby town. His age was showing, but his pleasant smile and gentle philosophy hadn't changed a bit.

"I'm not worrying about growing old," he said, coming out from under the hood. "Too busy enjoying life out here in the country. We've got three peach trees loaded with fruit and a hummingbird nestin' just outside our bedroom window. At twilight jackrabbits pop like corn out of the brush, and when the moon comes up, coyotes gather on the knoll and sing. I've never seen a spring with more abundant wildlife."

As she drove home, Jeanne thought about Mr. Simpson and his secret for happiness — Simpson's Special. Instead of dreading life's minuses, he made a habit of enjoying its pluses. It's like Earl Nightingale said: "Great attitude, great results; good attitude, good results; poor attitude, poor results." It rests with us to decide which one we'll have.

Sometimes having the right attitude can do more than simply enrich a life — sometimes it can save a life.

Jerry was the kind of guy who was always in a good mood, always smiling and joking. He was a natural motivator and a great restaurant manager. His employees loved him.

A friend of his once asked him what his secret was. He said, "Each morning I wake up and say to myself, 'Jerry, you have two choices today. You can choose to be in a good mood or you can choose to be in a bad mood.' I choose to be in a good mood. Each time something bad happens, I can choose to be a victim or I can choose to learn from it. I choose to learn from it. Every time someone comes to me complaining, I can choose to either listen passively or to help point out the positive side of life to them. I choose the positive side."

"But it's not that easy," Jerry's friend protested.

"Yes it is," Jerry said. "Life is all about choices. When you cut away all the junk, every situation is a choice. You choose how you react to circumstances. You choose how people will affect your frame of mind. You choose to be in a good mood or a bad mood. The bottom line: it's your choice how you live life."

A few years later Jerry forgot to lock the restaurant's back door late one night. Three armed men came in and held Jerry at gunpoint while they forced him to open the safe. His hand slipped from nervousness, and the robbers, panicking at the sudden move, shot him several times. Luckily, Jerry was found fairly quickly and rushed to a nearby trauma center. After many hours of delicate surgery and weeks in intensive care, Jerry was released from the hospital. He still had bullet fragments lodged in his body.

Several months later Jerry's friend saw him for the first time since the shooting. He asked him what had gone through his mind during those awful moments.

"The first thing that went through my mind is that I should've locked the back door," said Jerry with his customary humor. "Then, as I lay on the floor, I remembered that I had two choices: I could choose to live, or I could choose to die. I chose to live."

"Weren't you scared?" the friend asked.

"You bet," said Jerry. "The paramedics were great. They kept telling me I was going to be fine. But when they wheeled me into the emergency room and I saw the expressions on the faces of the doctors and nurses, I got really scared. In their eyes I could see that they already thought I was a dead man. I knew I needed to do something."

"What?"

"Well, there was this nurse shouting questions at me, asking me if I was allergic to anything. 'Yes!' I said. Everyone stopped working as they waited for my reply. I took a deep breath and said, 'Bullets!' Over their laughter, I told them, 'I'm choosing to live. Please operate on me like I'm alive, not dead.'"

Jerry lived thanks to the skill of his doctors — and thanks in no small part to his own attitude and resolve.

Jerry's story is a terrific example of the power of self-motivation. By making it a habit to first motivate ourselves we can learn how to effectively motivate others — employees, co-workers, clients, family and friends. Enthusiasm is contagious — and powerful. As Ralph Waldo Emerson said, "Every great and commanding moment in the annals of the world is a triumph of sound enthusiasm."

The very word "enthusiasm" alludes to its power. It's derived from the Greek *en*, meaning "in or within," and *theos*, meaning "God." So literally enthusiasm means "God within," a reference to its nobility and transformational ability. Without question it is one of man's strongest emotions. It motivates, it sparks creativity, it inspires, it reinforces self-confidence, it persuades, it clears the mind of negative thoughts.

So how can you jump-start your own engine? How can you tap your inner motivator? Three tools you can use are knowledge, self-affirmations and reading biographies of other successful people.

1) Knowledge. When we're proficient at something, we're naturally in a comfort zone. And *that* creates enthusiasm. Knowledge — about what we're doing and where we're going — can prompt us to take that vital first step in any endeavor. The willingness to take that step is the essence of self-motivation.

2) Self-Affirmations. On their surface, self-affirmations may seem like some of the most ridiculous activities possible for a rational adult mammal to engage in. But the simple fact is this: if we tell ourselves something often enough, pretty soon we'll start to believe it. The key is ensuring that we use positive self-affirmations instead of negative ones; it works both ways, remember. If we constantly remind ourselves how clumsy we are, *that's* the self-image we reinforce, and chances are we'll live up — or down — to those expectations.

Self-affirmations come in two flavors: soft and hard.

THE ONE PERCENT SOLUTION

Soft affirmations are designed to convince yourself of something over a period of time. You might, for example, tell yourself at least 10 times a day for 25 days, "I will read about leadership techniques for 30 minutes each day." The real power of the soft approach comes from the sincerity with which you set those goals. It's not a matter of forcing yourself to do something, but rather of persuading yourself that it's the right thing to do.

Hard affirmations are designed to pump you up. Try rolling out of bed each morning, standing up and saying loudly and enthusiastically, "I feel good, I feel great, and I'm ready to accelerate! I feel good, I feel great, and I'm ready to accelerate!"

Sound silly? Sure. But it *works* — provided, that is, that you really want it to work. One of my favorite self-affirmation stories concerns Jim Carrey. When he was still a struggling young comedian in California, he would drive into the Hollywood Hills late at night and stare down at the lights below. Then he would shout at the top of his voice, "I will earn $10 million a year by 1995!"

For several years Jim followed this seemingly ridiculous routine. But in 1995, he starred in a movie called *Ace Ventura: When Nature Calls* — and was paid $20 million. Of course his late night affirmations didn't make him a star — but they did keep him motivated and focused on his goal, and that's what made him a star.

Still sound silly? Here's a tip: don't worry about whether or not you believe your affirmation right away. Just focus on *wanting* to believe it. If you really want to believe it, eventually you will believe it — that's the magic of self-affirmations.

3) Read Biographies. Make a habit of studying the life stories of other people who overcame adversity to achieve success. Relating to these inspirational leaders makes success seem more attainable for us too. Success breeds success. When we read about someone like Winston Churchill or FDR, or hear about Michael Jordan's rigorous work ethic, or witness Mother Teresa's unselfish life of service in the Calcutta slums, we should be inspired to follow suit, to take action in our own lives. Inspiration is a powerful motivator.

Once we've learned to motivate ourselves, we're ready to motivate others. Enthusiasm is the single most effective tool for motivating others. Like I mentioned before, enthusiasm is infectious. Make that the foundation.

Enthusiasm alone isn't enough, however. Effective leaders are also knowledgeable, they respect the abilities and opinions of their employees, they make themselves available to hear complaints, suggestions or problems. They are supportive of others. They praise others often but sincerely. They are constructive in their feedback, never capricious or mean-spirited. They understand the concept of teamwork. They recognize that people are not simply interchangeable cogs in a machine, but marvelously unique and complex creatures with individual talents and goals.

THE ONE PERCENT SOLUTION

Captain Harry C. Butcher, General Eisenhower's naval aid during World War II, praised his commander's motivational skills: "The staff who worked with the General always felt motivated because he gave them consistent support and assistance when needed while still allowing them the freedom to use their own skills and knowledge. General Eisenhower's spirit of understanding inspired people and gave them the motivation necessary to work long hours in difficult situations."

Good leaders have the enviable ability of knowing how to bring out the best in people, of knowing how to make their followers feel special. And it's not just army generals or captains of industry who have that ability — sometimes it can be a simple school teacher.

Paul Harvey once told a story about just such a person. He called it "The Mouse that Roared":

Steve Morris wasn't a typical child; he knew it, and it made him unhappy. Like all kids, he just wanted to be normal. He just wanted to fit in.

His teacher, Mrs. Beneduci, was a wise woman who recognized Steve's sadness and realized that no matter what she said to him, mere words likely wouldn't make much of an impact on a nine-year-old. So she looked for some opportunity to show him how special he truly was. And one day, with the unlikely aid of a little gray mouse, she found it.

That morning she had called the class to order and said to them, "Children, we're going to follow a different schedule today — we're going to begin with history. I know you'd all rather be outside playing on such a beautiful day, but remember: if you never take the time to learn anything, all you'll know how to do is play."

When the class had settled down, Mrs. Beneduci asked, "Amy, who was Abraham Lincoln?"

Amy looked uncomfortable. She paused and fidgeted and finally whispered, " He, uh, he had, uh, a beard."

The rest of the class laughed, but many of them hadn't studied their history assignment either.

Mrs. Beneduci continued. "Steve, same question," she said.

Without hesitation Steve answered, "He was the 16th President of the United States."

"Very good," she said. "Now then, Abraham Lincoln was President during the Civil War . . ." She stopped as though she was listening to something. "What's that noise? Who's doing that?"

The puzzled class looked at each other. Steve sat quietly.

"I hear something that sounds like scratching. It sounds like a mouse," Mrs. Beneduci said.

Several little girls screamed, and several little boys laughed.

"Calm down, everyone," their teacher said. "It's not going to hurt you. It's probably just a little mouse. Steve, will you help me find it?"

Steve glowed with pride. He motioned for quiet, and cocked his ear, listening intently for a moment. "He's over there," Steve said, pointing at the wastebasket. "I hear him trying to get out."

Mrs. Beneduci quickly removed the little mouse from its wastebasket prison. Steve Morris had discovered it thanks to a remarkably acute sense of hearing — compensation, perhaps, for the fact that he had been born without sight.

The little mouse became a class mascot, and Steve became a popular boy. He was no longer ashamed of being blind — his gift of hearing was a constant source of wonder to the other children, and he became proud of his ability.

In time his marvelous ear helped make him a singer/composer/producer who won five Grammies, had 17 albums go gold and four go platinum. All because he could hear a little mouse moving around in a trashcan when no one else could. The confidence he gained from that one seemingly insignificant incident motivated him from that time forward to use his wonderful gift to the fullest. And from that time on, Steve Morris was known as Stevie Wonder.

Mrs. Beneduci demonstrated some terrific leadership skills. Knowing that words alone weren't enough to help Steve, she opened her mind and found a creative solution to a special situation.

Effective leaders recognize that no one is perfect. So they help people focus on their strengths. That fosters a sense of pride, accomplishment and confidence — which in turn help remedy any shortcomings. Good leaders know not only how to motivate others, but how to teach others to motivate themselves.

Andrew Carnegie, steel magnate and multi-millionaire,

once told a reporter his secret for bringing out the best in people. "Developing people is like mining for gold," he said. "When you mine for gold you might have to go through tons of dirt just to get one ounce of gold. But you don't look for dirt — you look for gold."

Conclusion

The right attitude is so often the difference between success and failure. As Milton said, "The mind can make a Heav'n of Hell, a Hell of Heav'n." Good leaders have good outlooks: they see opportunities where others see only obstacles, challenges where others see only problems.

Effective leaders know the value of enthusiasm. They create it in themselves through goal-oriented knowledge and self-affirmations, and by reading biographies of other successful leaders. They make a habit of positive thinking. They keep an open mind and know the value of learning from others' examples.

Good leaders win loyalty and spark enthusiasm in their employees by treating each of them with respect and friendship. They are sensitive to the strengths and weaknesses, goals and ambitions, hopes and fears of others. They strive constantly to bring out the best in their subordinates, professionally and personally.

THE ONE PERCENT SOLUTION

CH. 2 PERSONAL WORKSHEET

"Whether you think you can or think you can't, you are right."

— Henry Ford

How can I better my attitude by at least 1% by using the motivational tools I've just learned?

_____

_____

_____

_____

I will benefit by this 1% improvement in the following way:

_____

_____

_____

_____

CHAPTER 3

Get What You Want
The Fine Arts of Goal-Setting and Problem-Solving

*"People with goals succeed because they
know where they're going."*

— Earl Nightingale

Goal-setting seems, on its surface at least, to be a fairly simple procedure. Achieving those goals . . . well, that's when things get difficult. But setting them? Nah. Kid's stuff. Right?

Wrong. The fine art of goal-setting is a great deal more complex, and more important, than people expect. Setting high but still achievable goals tests a leader's logic, flexibility, realism, self-confidence and ambition.

Sure, it seems like anyone can decide on a goal. But only effective leaders are consistently able to set effective goals — goals that give maximum return for our investment of time, effort and resources. Those are the kind of goals that keep us competitive and innovative, that keep us moving in the right directions. Wrong-headed goals make us obsolete.

Take Swiss watches. Thirty years ago, the Swiss watch industry dominated nearly 70% of the world market, just as it had done for most of the century. Swiss watches were the best in the world, accurate and dependable.

The Swiss weren't content to simply rest on their laurels, either. They were constant innovators, always experimenting with new methods to make their watches even more accurate and dependable. They discovered better ways to manufacture the mainsprings, gears and bearings that composed the inner workings of a modern watch. They made great strides in waterproofing technology. They were at the top of the watchmaking pyramid, and seemed certain to remain there for a long, long time.

By 1980, though, their market share had fallen from almost 70% to less than 10%.

How? The quality of their watches hadn't diminished. Their goals of excellence and craftsmanship hadn't changed. They were still experimenting, trying to create the best self-winding watches possible.

And that was their failure. They were so focused on improving existing models that they couldn't see that the playing field had changed, that a new technology had rendered their superb craftsmanship and meticulous manufacturing obsolete. Self-winding mechanical watches had given way to new battery-powered digital watches.

What we call a paradigm shift had taken place. Suddenly it didn't matter one bit how proficient Swiss watchmakers were at producing gears and mainsprings. Electronic watches were the new standard, and the Swiss watch industry was unable to compete in such a radically changed market.

The Swiss watchmakers had set laudable goals for themselves: quality, consistent improvement, aesthetic perfection. But in the end, they had also set the wrong goals. Their focus was deep, but too narrow. They hadn't anticipated such a profound paradigm shift — worse, they never even tried to anticipate it. Their complacency doomed them to obsolescence and decline.

And that's why it's so vitally important not just that we make a habit of setting challenging goals for ourselves, but that we first learn to identify the right goals to set. If you're dying of thirst in the desert, and you know that water lies in one direction — and only one direction — chances are you're going to do everything in your power to spot which direction that is before you begin trudging up sand dunes.

Or think of it in less survivalist terms — a farmer planting a field, for instance. He doesn't simply scatter a random assortment of seeds across the ground, hoping that everything takes. No; he first takes some time and studies the acidity of the soil, the amount of sunlight the area receives, the amount of rainfall that he can expect and the range of temperatures for his part of the country.

He reads some books, looks at his neighbors' fields, talks to other successful farmers, sees what is already likely to grow well in the soil. Then he can identify not only the plants that should flourish under the conditions at hand, but also the plants that will give him the best return on his investment. All that prior preparation and study will obviously produce better and more consistent results that the random scatter approach.

And yet so often it's the scatter approach we employ in both our professional and personal lives. We latch onto goals that sound good, or seem easy, or promise us the world, without really considering whether or not they're the right goals to pursue, whether they're really practical, or attainable, or even good for us.

That's why we're so often disappointed with the results of our goal-setting. Too often we become discouraged at our lack of progress and simply quit, or, at the other extreme, we discover that the objective we've achieved isn't all that it was cracked up to be. Either way, we experience a kind of negative reinforcement hurts us the next time we try our hand at goal-setting.

We all know how easy it is to get excited about a new project — and how hard it is to maintain that same level of enthusiasm over time. We get frustrated by obstacles, or we get bored, or we get diverted by some other activity. Suddenly, we discover that the initial excitement that so galvanized us at the outset has faded, replaced by symptoms surprisingly reminiscent of the stages of grief.

First, there's the shock of potential failure. You may not think about it in quite those terms, but that's really what it is: you can't quite believe that things may not work out as rosily as you had planned. It's a blow to your ego, and you may not be able to absorb that right away.

Then there's denial — everything is going to be fine, nothing to worry about, no problem here. This isn't positive thinking, though — it's simply ignoring harsh realities instead of adapting to them.

The next stage is fear. What will happen if you fail? Will you lose your job? Your home? Your reputation? Will you be a laughingstock for having tried some screwy scheme in the first place?

So then you get angry. *Someone* caused you to fail; someone *wanted* you to fail. The world isn't fair. You didn't get a fair chance. Life stinks.

Then justification sets in. You rationalize away what's happening. It's not your fault. You did everything humanly possible. Maybe it wasn't such a good idea in the first place. Maybe this is all for the best . . .

And that thinking leads to an acceptance that you've failed. Maybe it still nags at you a little; maybe you're a little bitter about the experience. But you know that further struggle is useless. Time to move on.

So you start looking around for something else in which you can invest your energies. I call this the Grass Is Always Greener Syndrome. You cast about for other goals — and generally you end up glossing over their attendant difficulties. Everything else seems easier, more profitable, more attractive than the goal you're currently pursuing.

And at that point you have to make a choice: either to recommit to the goal at hand, or to commit to another one. If you make a habit of abandoning your goals this way, you'll never accomplish anything worth accomplishing — you'll simply bounce from project to project, accepting failure as a regular feature in your life. You'll never experience the intense satisfaction of facing obstacles and overcoming them instead of being daunted by them. Instead you'll make a habit of failure — and that's a hard habit to break.

So how can you do it? You simply have to learn more successful methods of identifying and achieving your goals. Then it's success, not failure, that becomes a habit.

Let's think about goal-setting in terms of problem-solving. After all, the reason we set goals in the first place is because we are, for any number of reasons, unsatisfied with the status quo. We want to move some aspect of our life from where it is now to where we would like it to be. Accomplishment denotes change — we want to change our lives for the better.

There's a causal link between a problem and the solution/goal we set. Problem: inadequate financial security. Goal: job promotion. Problem: lack of empowerment in the workplace. Goal: self-employment. Problem: feelings of underappreciation. Goal: achieving others' respect.

You get the idea. Goals are solutions. Solutions are goals.

So how can you know what solutions/goals are best for your circumstances? Here are some tips:

1. Define the problem. Unless you're able to clearly define the problem, your solution/goal will be equally muddled. And confusion, remember, leads only to failure.

GET WHAT YOU WANT

Success depends on clarity.

Bill and Julia were a happy young couple whose immediate goal was simple: they wanted Bill to earn enough to enable Julia to stay at home with their two little boys. Unfortunately, Bill's company couldn't afford to give him a raise, and he knew he wasn't likely to find a higher salary at another firm. Neither he nor Julia abandoned their goal, however.

As Bill drove home one afternoon after an especially tiring day, he decided to stop at a little roadside cafe for a while rather than risk falling asleep at the wheel. While he nursed a cup of coffee he overheard a group of golfers complaining about the number of balls they were losing in water hazards at several nearby courses.

Things suddenly clicked in place for Bill. His passion was scuba diving, and he was an excellent swimmer. He saw an opportunity. Forgetting his fatigue, he drove to a nearby pro shop and talked the manager into allowing him a chance to dive for lost golf balls. Then he scoured the bottom of just one of the many small lakes that dotted most Florida golf links.

He saw that the lake bottom was almost solid white with lost balls. He brought up a batch and examined them in daylight. Most looked like new, and the manager offered to buy them. Bill agreed, then brought up another 200 balls before calling it a day.

Soon virtually all of Bill's free time was spent diving for balls on golf courses throughout the region. The possibilities seemed so great that Bill quit his job so he could recover balls full-time. Julia helped by cleaning the used balls and sorting them by make and quality. Within a year Bill was known as the Used Golf Ball King of Florida, earning enough to allow Julia to stay home with their children. Their dream had come true.

Bill and Julia were successful because they were creative, hard-working and opportunistic. They were also very clear about their problem (not enough income) and their subsequent goal (enough money to allow Julia to stay home). With those constantly in mind, they were always in search of potential solutions, and able to spot and seize the right one when it presented itself.

2. Identify the source of the problem. It's important that we understand how and why a problem exists. Identifying the source takes critical analysis, insight and honesty. Is our boss really the problem? Or is it that we feel threatened by his youth or education? Are we really unappreciated? Or are we just feeling sorry for ourselves? Do we need more income? Or is it just our reckless spending habits that need adjusting?

For any solution to be truly effective, it has to deal with the root causes. Physicians treat the disease, not the symptoms. In the same way we have to learn to diagnose the underpinning problem and set goals for solving it, not its superficialities.

3. Explore possible solutions. Creativity is an invaluable part of the problem-solving/goal-setting process. Consider the lesson of Jan Milligan's account in "The Lampshade Problem":

"Three of us pilots watched from the cockpit of our Boeing 727 as a woman boarded the plane with a lampshade on her head. We made wild guesses about the reason, and then, since I was the junior pilot, I was assigned the job of finding out.

" 'If I checked it as luggage, it would've been smashed,' the lady said in response to my question. 'If I carried it on board, the flight attendant would've asked me to stuff it under my feet or squeeze it into the overhead bin. So I just wore it, and no one said a word.' "

Creativity requires flexibility and open-mindedness, and it sure helps to be able to turn a problem on its head and examine it from another angle. So often we underestimate how important our vantage point is in the whole problem-solving process.

That's well-illustrated in Susan Crockett's story:

"One of my favorite hobbies is flea marketing. I love a bargain but rarely feel comfortable dickering with the seller. A wonderful opportunity finally arose at a sale when I spotted a beautiful set of water goblets that was missing a glass. That gave me the perfect bargaining tool.

"I said to the seller, 'Too bad there's no eighth goblet in the set.'

" 'Lady,' he replied, 'this is a set of six glasses. There's just an extra in case one ever gets broken.' "

You say tomato, I say tomato. Make it a habit to be open-minded.

There's been a lot of work in recent years about the role each side of the brain plays in problem-solving. Briefly, the left hemisphere of the brain controls our logic and verbal functions. It deals with words, with parts and specifics. It controls analysis (breaking things up) and sequential thinking.

The right hemisphere, in contrast, is our intuitive and creative center. It deals with pictures and images, with the relationship between parts. It controls our ability to synthesize (put together) ideas and think holistically about things.

Neither side of the brain is "better" than the other — each has a role to play in decision making and problem-solving. Be flexible. Remember what the psychologist Abraham Maslow once said: "He that's good with a hammer tends to think everything is a nail."

4. Decide on the best resolution. After considering a host of possibilities, the time inevitably comes for you to choose one. Don't be afraid to be decisive! This is where your research, open-mindedness and creativity pay off.

5. Take action! Action is key. Remember: leaders are doers. Not talkers, or whiners, or dreamers, or thinkers. Talking, dreaming and thinking all have their place (not whining, though), but in the final analysis it's the action that separates effective leaders from would-be leaders. Don't let the fear of making the wrong choice prevent you from making any choice.

Franklin Roosevelt said, "It is common sense to take a method and try it. If it fails, admit it frankly and try another. But above all try *something*."

The optimal solution isn't always the obvious solution — at least to you. Sometimes other people, other points of view, can help you discover the best path. That's what happened in Shirley Bacheler's story, "Angel on a Doorstep."

Shirley had recently moved to a small town, a peaceful idyllic spot where, among other things, milkmen still brought bottles of milk right up to the doorstep. It was a chilly November, so Shirley was glad the milk deliveries saved her additional trips to the grocery store. Besides, she enjoyed the cheerful small talk with her milkman, Ben.

One day, however, she couldn't help but notice that Ben was the epitome of gloom. After some careful, sympathetic questioning she found out the reason.

It seems that two of Ben's customers had left town without paying their bills, and the losses would have to come out of his own pocket. One bill was only for about $10, but the other was for a whopping $79. Neither customer had left a forwarding address, and Ben was especially angry at himself for letting the second bill grow so large.

"She was a pretty woman with six children and another

on the way," he said. "She was always saying she'd pay soon, that her husband was looking for a second job. I believed her. I thought I was doing a good thing, but instead I've been had."

All Shirley could think to say was, "I'm so sorry."

The next time Shirley saw Ben, his anger seemed even worse. She again sympathized with him, but found herself thinking about his situation long after he'd dropped off the milk and left. She knew how anger and anxiety like Ben's could embitter a person forever.

Then she remembered some advice her grandmother had once given her: "If someone takes something from you, give it to him instead. You can never be robbed that way."

When Ben next came around, Shirley told him her idea. "Give the woman that milk," she advised. "Make it a Christmas present to those kids who needed it."

"Are you kidding?" he said. "I can't afford to give my wife a present that expensive!"

"Remember the Bible says, 'I was a stranger and you took Me in.' You just took her in with all her little children," Shirley said.

"Don't you mean she took me in?"

But Ben took Shirley's advice to heart, and when she saw him next he seemed more cheerful, more like his old self. "I did it," he told her. "I gave her the milk as a Christmas present. It wasn't easy, but hey — what did I have to lose? It was gone anyway."

"Yes, but you've got to really mean it in your heart," she

said.

"I know, and I really do feel better," Ben answered. "Those kids had lots of milk just because of me."

The holidays came and went. One January morning Shirley saw Ben grinning from ear to ear as he walked up to her door.

"Wait till you hear this," he said. He explained that he'd been covering for another milkman on a different route when he heard someone calling his name. He saw an woman running towards him waving something, and realized that it was the same woman who hadn't paid her bill.

"Ben, wait a minute! I've got some money for you," she had said. "I'm so sorry it's so late. I've been meaning to find you." She explained that her husband had found a place with cheaper rent and that he'd also secured a night job. The family had moved quickly and forgotten to leave a forwarding address. "Here's $20 towards our bill."

"That's all right," Ben had said. "It's been paid."

"Paid?" she had asked. "But how? Who?"

"Well, I did," he had told her.

She had burst into tears.

"What did you do then?" Shirley asked him.

Ben smiled a little bashfully and said, "I didn't know what to do. Before I knew it I was crying too. I thought about all those kids and . . . well, I'm just glad you talked me into doing that."

"So, did you take the $20?" Shirley asked.

"Of course not," he said indignantly. "I gave her that milk

as a present, didn't I!"

Make sure that whatever solution you decide on, it's one that lets you sleep peacefully at night. But remember to implement some solution. As Lee Iacocca said, "Solutions come from many people and places, but every individual needs to remember this basic fact: don't talk things to death. Act. Action is what brings solutions!"

And keep acting. Don't give up. Don't quit because you can't see any immediate results. "If you have a dream, go after it, and keep on keeping on," Peter Michelmore taught his students. "You'll come through to a desirable solution."

Wayne Dyer, the author of the bestselling *Your Erroneous Zones*, didn't achieve instant success with his book. But he had a plan — and the faith that by sticking to it he would eventually succeed. He self-printed copies of the book and trudged from town to town, publisher to publisher, with them. He appeared on local late-night, non-primetime radio talk shows — strictly small-fry stuff, true, but those were the venues that were willing to book him, and he figured that any exposure was a good thing.

His plan paid off. One night on just such a show in San Francisco, who should be listening but Johnny Carson. Carson loved the book and invited Dyer to appear on his show, and the rest is history. Sure, Dyer was lucky — but in large part he made his own luck. He weighed his options, decided on the best course and stuck to it.

GET WHAT YOU WANT

Now that we've talked about problem-solving as a means of identifying both goals and the means to achieve them, let's look at some other ways to help us become more effective goal-setters.

1. Make your goals challenging but still believable. We've already talked about the necessity of choosing the right goals. Part and parcel of that is having the maturity to know what's attainable and what's not. Setting unrealistic goals gives us a built-in excuse to fail.

On the other hand, without challenge there can be no growth. We should constantly be exploring our limits, expanding our horizons, testing ourselves. Challenge creates excitement and brings out the best in us.

Set goals you honestly intend on accomplishing, but don't be afraid to push yourself. Remember Casey Kacem's famous tag line: "Keep your feet on the ground, but keep reaching for the stars!"

2. Put your goals in writing. In 1953 Yale University surveyed its graduating class and discovered that only three percent had written goals. Twenty years later, Yale surveyed the same group and learned that those three percent who had taken the time to actually write down their goals had amassed a net worth greater than the other 97% combined.

Putting your goals in writing helps your focus, your motivation and your determination. If you feel a little silly about doing it, remember that no one need know except you.

And also remember that in doing so, you're demonstrating a commitment that separates you from the rest of the pack and betters your odds of success by a significant amount. And that's nothing to be embarrassed about.

3. Set specific objectives. There's no substitute for a well-developed plan. Former Notre Dame head coach Lou Holtz said, "You transform yourself from being one of life's spectators into being a real participant by setting goals and consistently working towards them. Strongly-held wishes do not qualify. Leadership comes from specific objectives that may become concrete action."

Napoleon Hill, who spent 20 years studying the habits and attitudes of successful people, was just as emphatic: "Analysis of several hundred people who had accumulated fortunes disclosed the fact that they had definite goals during the whole climb toward success."

Broad, generalized goals are nice — but they're not enough. Remember the old saying: "The devil is in the details." So is success.

4. Use short-term goals to achieve long-term success. There's nothing wrong with setting long-term goals, but there's no question that the further away a goal is from being realized, the harder it is to maintain enthusiasm and commitment over time. One way to help mitigate that is to set several short-term goals. The satisfaction of achieving them will boost your morale and help keep you moving towards your ultimate objective.

Here's a great story about how using short term measurable successes can lead to amazing transformations:

Sonny was a young man who grew up in Austria. He was a skinny kid and was frequently teased about his lack of stature. Finally, he decided he'd had enough. He threw himself into a weight-lifting and workout program, going to the local gym three times and week and exercising every evening at home.

He set short-term goals for himself, and considered it a victory every time he increased the amount of weight on the bar or the number of sit-ups he did. He was extremely disciplined, and refused to let anything interrupt his workout schedule. Soon no one called Sonny skinny.

In time, Sonny became a professional bodybuilder and won several titles before trying his hand at acting. And today Arnold (Sonny) Schwarzenegger is one of the world's most successful box office stars, as well as a happy husband, father and businessman.

5. Constantly evaluate where you're going. This is the flip side to the advice given above. Short-term goals are a great motivator, but it's equally important never to lose sight of our ultimate ambition. It's easy sometimes to become so fixated on the details that we forget exactly why it is that we're doing what we're doing.

Steven Covey said, "Effective people follow a thoughtful course. They understand that it is incredibly easy to get caught up in an activity trap of climbing the ladder of success only to discover it is leaning against the wrong wall."

Effective leaders strive for balance between short-term goals and long-term objectives. Visualize yourself walking through the mountains — you want to keep checking the horizon to ensure that you're heading in the right direction, but you also want to keep your eyes on the ground in front of you to make sure you don't stumble off a cliff.

6. Adjust your goal when necessary. Sometimes circumstances change, and as they do, we have to have the flexibility to change with them. Rigidity is confining. It limits our choices and subsequently our potential for success — as the Swiss watchmakers discovered to their chagrin.

A battleship assigned to a training squadron had been at sea on maneuvers for several days in heavy weather. As night fell a patchy fog rolled in, so the captain stayed on the bridge instead of going below.

A little while later, the lookout reported, "Light bearing on the starboard bow!"

"Is it steady or moving astern?" the captain asked.

"Steady, sir."

The captain knew that meant the two were on a collision course. He called his signalman. "Signal that ship: *We are on a collision course, advise you change course 20 degrees.*"

Back came a signal: *"Advisable for you to change course 20 degrees."*

The captain said, "Send: *I'm a captain, change course 20*

degrees."

Again the response: *"I'm a seaman second class, change course 20 degrees."*

The captain was furious. "Send: *I'm a battleship, change course 20 degrees."*

Back came the flashing light: *"I'm a lighthouse."*

The captain changed course.

It's great to be determined, but stubbornness is no virtue. In both our professional and our personal lives we have to know when to stay the course — and when to change course.

Judy Bodmer gave a very different account of the need — and the satisfaction — of knowing when to shift priorities in her story, "Confessions of a Sports Mom":

"It's a chilly Saturday in May. I am sitting on a cold seat in a baseball stand when my son's coach calls to me as he passes.

" 'Mrs. Bodmer, I'm starting your son today in right field. He deserves the opportunity; he's worked hard this year.'

"I'm proud of my son; I'm glad his hard work is being rewarded. As the team members trot onto the field, I search for my son's number. It isn't there. Instead, Eddie, the most inexperienced player on the team, takes right field. I want to run over and ask the coach what's going on, but I know Mathew wouldn't like that.

"My son is gripping the chain-link fence in front of the dugout and yelling encouragement to his teammates. My heart breaks because I know how disappointed he must be. I don't understand what drives boys to put themselves through this.

" 'Atta boy, Eddie!" yells his father. He is proud that his son is starting. I've seen this same man walk out of games in disgust when his son dropped a ball or made a bad throw, but now he is proud.

"In the fourth inning Mathew is called to bat. He takes a couple of practice swings. I yell encouragement. It is easy to see that he is trying, but he strikes out. My son hangs his head as he walks back to the dugout; I wish I could help him.

"People may wonder why a parent would go through this. It's not because I want to fulfill my dream of excelling at sports through my kids. I also don't do this for the emotional highs, though I've had some. I've seen my sons score winning goals in soccer, hit home runs in baseball and spark come-from-behind wins in basketball. Mostly, though, I've seen heartaches. I've sat in the stands year after year observing it all and wondering why.

"The game ends. The coach meets with the team. They yell some rallying cry and then descend on their parents. I notice Eddie's dad has a big grin as he slaps his son on the back. Mathew wants to get a drink. While I wait for him, the coach approaches me.

" 'Mrs. Bodner, I want you to know that's a fine young man you have there.'

" 'Why?' I ask, waiting for him to explain why he broke my son's heart.

"He continued, 'When I told Mathew he could start, he

thanked me and turned me down. He told me to let Eddie start since it was so important to him.'

"As I watched Mathew come toward me I understood why I sit in the stands where I can watch my sons — where I can watch them adjust their goals as they grow into men to be proud of."

Conclusion

It's not enough to simply be goal-oriented. To be effective leaders we have to be *right*-goal-oriented — we have to learn to identify and pursue the appropriate goals.

Goal-setting and problem-solving are closely related. Ultimately solving problems brings us closer to achieving our goals, so it's important that we learn to deal with them effectively by recognizing the problems, identifying their source, exploring possible solutions and finally deciding on and carrying out the best available solution. Action is key.

To better our chances of achieving the goals we set for ourselves, we should make them challenging but attainable, take the time to write them down, set specific objectives, use short-term goals to keep us motivated towards long-term ambitions, regularly reevaluate and, if necessary, readjust our goals.

Productive leaders have learned to devote their energies towards productive goals, deriving maximum return for their efforts. They've made successful goal-setting a habit — and that means they've made a habit of success.

THE ONE PERCENT SOLUTION

CH. 3 PERSONAL WORKSHEET

"The great thing in this world is not so much where we are, but in what direction we are going."

— Oliver Wendell Holmes

What is one action I can take to improve my goal-setting/problem-solving skills by at least 1%?

_____

_____

_____

_____

I will benefit by this 1% improvement in the following way:

_____

_____

_____

_____

CHAPTER 4

Sticking with It

The Role of Persistence in Success

*"Genius is one percent inspiration and 99 percent
perspiration. I never did anything worth doing
by accident. They came by work."*

— Thomas Edison

When I arrived in the U.S. to attend university, the
first job I found was as a pizza delivery driver. Truthfully, I
was excited about the prospect of earning a whole $2.75 an
hour, plus 25¢ per delivery (it was the 70s, after all), and I
quickly became the most efficient driver the restaurant had.

Since, at least in the pizza business, efficiency equals
speed, that also means I was the fastest driver around (no
immigrant taxi driver jokes, please), and occasionally I ran
afoul of local police speed traps. One time the officer who
pulled me over actually asked me why I was in such a hurry.
I didn't even have to think about my response: "Sir, if I don't
hurry, my customers are going to end up with cold pizza."

He tried not to smile and didn't quite succeed. "Son," he said, "last time I checked, delivering pizzas wasn't a national emergency."

Well, it was to me, I thought as I drove away. I figured every pizza was important, every customer was special. I knew that there were more pressing things in life, but I had no control over those. What I could do — what I was determined to do — was to ensure that every single paying customer of Valentino's Pizza received a hot pizza pie.

My attitude paid off. Soon I was promoted, first to kitchen staff, then shift-manager and eventually manager. I was feeling pretty good about my progress, proud of my dedication and determination, pleased with my success.

Then the roof fell in.

Not literally, of course, and not all at once, either. On the surface, the restaurant was doing a respectable business. Behind the scenes, however, it seems that the owner was diligently mismanaging what should have been a solid going concern, squandering what profits there were, neglecting to pay our vendors or the good folks at the IRS.

So after a few months of dodging, we were informed by the IRS that the overdue taxes had better be paid immediately (if not sooner) or they would foreclose. The owner saw no way out of the hole into which he had dug himself. He had given up, but I saw an opportunity.

I offered to pay off the current owner's debts in exchange for ownership of the pizza parlor, a deal he happily agreed to. Over the next couple of weeks I persuaded Uncle Sam and our less powerful (but no less persistent) vendors to restructure our debts so I could pay it off over the course of a year's time. I put college on hold so all my energies could be brought to bear on saving the restaurant. I might not have had all my eggs in one basket, but that's only because in all hustle I probably forgot one or two. It certainly wasn't for lack of trying.

For the next year I worked harder than I had ever worked in my life. I felt like a storm-tossed ship — just when it seemed that the worst had passed, another wave, even bigger than its predecessors, would rise up out of nowhere to batter me again. I began to wonder if Somebody was out to get me. It had all seemed so easy on paper. At times, sometimes fairly often, I thought about quitting.

The crisis came one rain-soaked night. One of my drivers never showed up, and another's car broke down. Orders were brisk, and it seemed like there was no way we could satisfy all our customers. I was a nervous wreck.

Somehow we muddled through that hellish shift. But I was physically and emotionally exhausted. After the employees had all gone home and I had closed the restaurant, I stood in the darkened office, alone. And suddenly all that anger and frustration and worry and fear erupted, and I screamed aloud.

And I have to admit, I felt a little better. And then I thought about the things that I had accomplished, the positive things I would be throwing away if I just quit. I thought about how I had started, a lowly delivery driver, and how elated I had been about my very first promotion. And how there had been the even bigger thrill of becoming manager. And I remembered how I had lain awake the first night after I bought the business, my mind alive not with the prospect of future difficulties, but of future opportunities. And I thought that quit is, when you boil it down, a dirty, demeaning word.

My little heart-to-heart with myself gave me the renewed determination not to simply walk away. I decided to stick it out, trusting that my hard work wouldn't be in vain and that things would get better. And if they didn't, well then, I figured at least I'd go down swinging.

My persistence was well-placed. Within a year, sales had increased by 700%, I'd paid off all our debts, and the university newspaper had declared Valentino's the best pizza joint in town. We had crested the hump, and looking back on it, I can't tell you how glad I am that I didn't let myself be overwhelmed by frustration and negativism that horrible stormy night. It would have been so easy to quit, so easy to have just abandoned all my hopes and dreams for the business simply because I didn't feel up to the challenges of ownership.

The most costly phrase in the English language is, "I don't feel like it." It's tempting to give in to it, to avoid responsibilities we don't feel we have time for, to avoid obstacles we don't feel like surmounting, to avoid bruised egos we don't feel like sustaining. Most projects fail, professional and personal alike, not because of some direct outside force, but because at some point we decide to quit—or rather, not to succeed. What we're really saying is, "I don't feel like succeeding." And that's just plain silly.

Here's one of my favorite passages: "Nothing in the world can take the place of persistence. Talent will not — nothing is more common than unsuccessful men with talent. Genius will not — unrewarded genius is almost a proverb. Education will not — the world is full of educated derelicts. Persistence and determination alone are omnipotent."

Determination doesn't come easily, though. You can't buy it, you can't inherit it, you can't lend or borrow it. It's got to come from within. You've got to discover it somewhere inside yourself and nurture it through the proverbial blood, sweat and tears.

It's like a sculptor working with a block of marble — he doesn't create a statue, he simply skillfully frees the statue that, to his eyes at least, is already present but hidden from ordinary view. You — all of us — can unlock the truly awesome power of your own determined will the same way, first by recognizing its existence within you, and then by taking the time to chisel away all the hang-ups, the I-don't-feel-like-its, the fears and anxieties that keep it trapped.

Let's take closer look at some of the tools we can use to shape our inner determination:

1. Clarity of purpose
2. Self-confidence
3. Persistence
4. Self-discipline

Clarity of Purpose

Know exactly what you want and visualize yourself achieving it — positive reinforcement really works. Daily life too often prompts us to diffuse our energies in a vain attempt to deal with a dozen little crises. A single clear, well-defined challenge can help us focus all our energies more tightly on the task at hand. Henry Ford once said, "Leadership skills are grounded in a desire to excel. Excelling can be accomplished most easily if a clear challenge is apparent."

In visualizing your goals, don't be afraid to set high standards for yourself. Making a habit of striving consistently for excellence is a wonderful reinforcer. As Corrie ten Boom reminded her readers in her essay, "Each New Day": "There is no neutrality on the battle line between good and best. Work only for the best in all your efforts."

Working for the best doesn't mean, however, that your goals have to be lofty or complicated. Every journey begins with a single step — every life can profit from making even a 1% change for the better. Here's a wonderful story about how setting — and achieving — a simple but well-defined goal can nonetheless lead to unexpected rewards:

One blustery Saturday afternoon in January, 1989, Susan Sharp and her eight-year-old son David were trudging across a snow-covered parking lot in Chippawa Falls, Wisconsin, on their way home from a shopping trip. Suddenly Susan's cane slipped on an ice-patch and she sprawled face-first into the slush.

David immediately rushed over. "Are you OK, Mom?" he

asked.

"I'm fine, honey," Susan said as she shakily rose to her feet. "I'm OK."

It had been nearly two years since Susan had been diagnosed with multiple sclerosis, and she was falling more frequently now, even in good conditions. In winter things were even worse, and every ice-patch represented a potential bone fracture.

David wished he could help somehow, but, he thought bitterly, he couldn't even help himself. The second-grader had a speech impediment. It embarrassed him, and at school he rarely asked questions or read aloud. Although a bright, inquisitive boy, he was becoming more isolated from his classmates and dropping further behind in his schoolwork.

Not long after his mother's fall in the parking lot, David's teacher gave the class a special assignment: she wanted each student to build an invention and enter it in Invent America, a national contest sponsored by U.S. businesses and designed to help foster creativity in children. David thought about what he could do, but every idea he had seemed too complicated for an eight-year-old to construct.

Then, one night while he watched his mother in the kitchen, he remembered her fall in the parking lot. Suddenly an inspiration struck him: what if he could make her cane slip-proof? He rushed over to her and pointed at the cane.

"Mom, you remember how you're always falling on the ice? What if I fixed your cane so a nail poked out the bottom?"

"But the sharp end will scratch the floor," Susan said.

David thought for a moment. "I could make it like a ball-point pen," he said. "You'd have a button in the handle, and when you pressed it you could make the nail pop in and out."

A few days later David (with his father's help) finished the modified cane. They watched as Susan used it to shuffle up and down the icy driveway. "It's wonderful," she said. "I didn't slip at all."

That July, David won first prize at the national Invent America awards ceremony in Washington, D.C. On the plane trip back home, he met a woman from Minnesota who also had multiple sclerosis. When he excitedly told her about his invention, she asked him if he'd make a similar cane for her. He agreed.

Soon orders for David's special canes came pouring in. His self-confidence soared, as did his ability to communicate clearly — he was getting a lot of practice, after all. Within a few years he was nearly free of his speech impediment, and his invention was awaiting patent approval. His simple goal had bloomed into an unexpected success, helping hundreds of grateful people — including himself.

Self-Confidence

We talked a few chapters ago about learning to expand our comfort zones in order to increase our confidence in our own abilities. There's no question that a firm belief that we *can* accomplish something is a necessary foundation to actually achieving that thing. The Roman poet Virgil taught his listeners, "People can conquer when they believe they can."

Building self-confidence is a gradual process, and usually personal experience proves the best teacher. Drawing on past experiences, especially on past successes, is invaluable. I still look back to the trials, and eventual triumph, of my time as a pizza restaurateur whenever I face some new challenge. I remember the seemingly insurmountable obstacles that, through hard work, creativity and perseverance, I was able to overcome. If I did it then, I know that I can do it again. I can succeed.

And so can you.

Perseverance

Self-confidence is a great asset. Marry it to perseverance and you've got a practically unbeatable combination. Here's the record of one leader whose life was never without adversity, whose career was never without setbacks, but who persevered nevertheless:

He failed in business at age 31.
He lost a bid for the state legislature at age 32.
He failed again in business at age 34.
He faced the death of a sweetheart at age 35.
He had a nervous breakdown at age 36.
He lost another election at age 38.

THE ONE PERCENT SOLUTION

He lost congressional races at ages 43, 46 and 48.

He lost a senatorial race at age 55.

He lost a bid for the Vice-Presidency at age 56.

He lost another senatorial race at age 58.

At age 60, Abraham Lincoln was elected President of the United States.

Elbert Hubbard once wrote, "There is no failure except in no longer trying." Everyone faces rejections — ask any writer. John Grisham said he could wallpaper his house with the number of rejection letters he received before selling his first manuscript. The same is true of authors as diverse as F. Scott Fitzgerald, Dr. Seuss, Louis L'Amour, William Saroyan, Tom Clancy, Stephen King and Jack London. But none of them gave up, and by believing in their talent and persevering, all have become remarkably successful professional authors. On another note, a recent survey showed that the average self-made millionaire has failed in business an *average* of 17 times before striking it rich.

Perseverance feeds off self-confidence, and in turn helps foster it. There's a story about Thomas Edison in which he's asked by a reporter why he's continuing his efforts to perfect the light bulb, even though he's tried thousands of variations without success.

"Mr. Edison," the reporter asked, "why do you insist on pursuing this notion? You're in danger of ruining your reputation — after all, it's perfectly obvious that if you can't make it work after 10,000 tries, you'll never make it work. It's impossible."

"Young man," Edison rumbled, "what you fail to understand is that I haven't failed 10,000 times. On the contrary, I have successfully identified 10,000 ways a light bulb will not work. Now all I need to do is to identify one way that it will."

I think I can safely say that we're all thankful he continued that search.

Self-Discipline

I was always amazed at my grandmother's patience in dealing with difficult people and difficult situations. She never seemed flustered, never lost her temper. I once asked her how she did it.

"I decided early in life that I'd make a list of others' faults that I'd forgive without hesitation," she said.

When I asked to see the list, she just smiled.

"To tell you the truth, I never did get around to making that list," she said. "But whenever people say or do something that upsets me, I tell myself that that's the very thing I would've put at the top of it."

The kind of self-discipline my grandmother displayed in refusing to lose her calm can serve all of us well. Self-discipline is a valuable check on our more volatile emotions, preventing them from getting out of hand. It makes us mature, responsible adults, capable of constructive communication and productive sustained action.

THE ONE PERCENT SOLUTION

Self-image guru Zig Ziglar says, "The key to building a healthy self-image is self-discipline. The individuals who have self-discipline are in control to do what they need to do when they need to do them. Such persons will extend themselves by acquiring knowledge from every situation they experience."

We all know people whose excitement at the beginning of a new project is unparalleled. They practically brim over with ideas, optimism and positive energy. But then, three weeks later, they're nowhere to be seen. Their initial enthusiasm has flagged in the face of hard work and delayed gratification. The first series of setbacks sends them scurrying back to their cubicles, dismayed and discouraged — until the next time they get excited about something.

It's just common sense that most goals worth achieving can't be achieved right away. It takes time to accomplish them. And it's somewhere between that initial resolve and the end result that most of us, most of the time, just sort of fade away. We get bored, or we don't see any positive change, or we get discouraged, or we get tired, or we get diverted, or we let life get in the way.

Dieting and exercise routines are prime examples of projects that test our stick-to-it-tiveness. We start with the best of intentions — and only afterward realize the willpower necessary to follow through. And, as I know from personal experience, your willpower is generally stronger when you're happy, comfortable and . . . well, awake. Here's my tale:

Until last year I had never been a runner. But, in an effort to stay fit, I decided to start running regularly. I enrolled in a training program called Austin Fit. Every Saturday morning a group of novice runners like me got together for a bout of stretching, a short seminar on running tips and techniques and a long run.

To make the most of the Saturday sessions, I planned to run four to six miles three to five times a week. The catch was that my already overcrowded schedule didn't allow for a great deal of exercise time . . . unless I woke up at 5:30 in the morning to do it.

It sounded good on paper, but I definitely had second thoughts when the Hour of Doom actually arrived. I blearily stared at my alarm clock and wondered if I wouldn't be just as happy, and a whole lot more rested, if I just rolled back under the covers and caught another 40 winks . . . or 80, for that matter.

But I forced myself out of bed and started the work-out, tousled, upset and embittered that others were still sleeping the sleep of the just while I achily pounded away along the pavement. Gradually, though, those feelings melted away, and by the end of my first run I felt energized, awake and actually refreshed. I was glad that I had made the decision to do it after all.

Not that that made it any easier to get up the next morning, mind you.

Still, I forced myself to stick with it despite the temptations to the contrary. Curiously, after I'd been on the program for a while, I found that if I did miss a run I felt guilty and disappointed. And eventually the results that I had been waiting for began to make themselves felt. I was in better shape, I had a better frame of mind, I had more energy and creativity. And I ran — and finished — the 3M half-marathon a few months later.

Another benefit of self-discipline is that it keeps us firmly focused on the present. While the past is a valuable teacher, too often it's also a repository of guilt. While the future is filled with opportunity, too often it's also attended by doubt and anxiety. The emotional energy we waste dwelling on past mistakes or worrying about future uncertainties could be so much more productively spent making the most of the present.

Wayne Dyer wrote, "Healthy, fulfilled people are free from guilt and all the attendant anxiety that goes with using any present moments in being immobilized by past events. Certainly such persons can admit to making mistakes, and they can vow to avoid repeating certain behaviors that are counterproductive in any way, but they do not waste their time wishing that they had not done something."

We don't drive our cars looking through the rearview mirror. Neither can we focus our vision on what's happening three streets down. We've got to be present-oriented, dealing with the here and now, with the things we actually have some control over. Guilt only gnaws away at our self-confidence; anxiety paralyzes our clear thinking. As doers, we should concentrate on doing, not on worrying.

Conclusion

Tenacity is an essential leadership quality. Everyone, sooner or later, is faced squarely with some crisis, and only by gritting our teeth and pushing through, determined not to fail, can we reach our potential. We can help strengthen our own sense of determination by being clear about our purpose, by having confidence in ourselves and by being perseverant and disciplined.

Effective leaders know that goals don't necessarily have to be complex, that they can draw strength from past experiences to combat the challenges facing them today, and that short-term setbacks should not imperil their long-term objectives. They also recognize the value of disciplining their emotions, and understand the futility of worrying about the past or future. Good leaders are good doers.

THE ONE PERCENT SOLUTION

CH. 4 PERSONAL WORKSHEET

"Never give in, never give in, never, never, never, never — in nothing, great or small, large or petty — never give in except to convictions of honor and good sense."

— Winston Churchill

I will become more persistent by at least 1% by choosing not to give up on this one goal:

_____

_____

_____

_____

I will benefit by this 1% improvement in the following way:

_____

_____

_____

_____

CHAPTER 5

Treasure Each Moment

Lessons in Effective Time Management

*"Use no other man's time for
you never can replace it."*

— William Shakespeare

Let's just say, for the sake of the topic at hand, that you're 30 years old. (I'm willing to bet a lot of you already like where this train is going.) There's a catch, though.

At age 30 you've already lost 262,800 hours of your life. That time is gone forever, never to be replaced or relived, only remembered. (For mercy's sake I won't tell you how many hours you've lost at 45 — if you're really that morbidly curious you can do the math yourself.) The point is this: Life is precious. Life is fragile. Don't waste it.

I learned that lesson the hard way. Long ago, when I was a teenager growing up in Iran, I had an experience that taught me about the inherent uncertainty of life, about the illusion of complacency.

One day, while still in high school, I was called into the principal's office. I didn't remember having done anything wrong, so I wasn't particularly worried. The principal told me that some men from Savak, the Shah's secret police, wanted to talk to me about a student organization I was president of — sort of a cross between student council and the Boy Scouts. Not having anything to hide, I was still blissfully unconcerned. Probably routine, I thought. At worst, some easily cleared-up misunderstanding. No problem. At least I'd get out of class for a while.

The principal drove me to a large, undistinguished-looking building. There were no signs or markings anywhere on it. My principal escorted me inside, and then nervously turned to go. That's when the first warning bell went off inside my head.

"Hey, how am I going to get back?" I asked him.

"Aah . . . don't worry," he called over his rapidly retreating shoulder. "I'll be back to get you later." I wasn't reassured. I began to worry.

Some time later I was taken to a small, bare room and told to wait. Thirty minutes passed. An hour. An hour and a half. Finally the door opened and a couple of deadly serious, completely humorless men came in. Without even an introduction they launched into a series of strange and frightening questions:

What had I done on such and such date?

Who was I with at such and such time?

TREASURE EACH MOMENT

What was the nature of my relationship to such and such person?

They asked me all sorts of mysterious questions, but refused to answer even one of mine, especially the most pressing one, "Why am I here?" I still had no idea what, if anything, I had done wrong.

I don't remember exactly how long the questioning went on. A long time — that I'm sure of. Finally one of the men opened the door and motioned to someone outside. Two hulking thugs with machine guns came in. They grabbed me, forced my arms behind my back, and handcuffed me. I thought the worst was about to happen. I thought I was about to die, shot in the back of the head in some anonymous holding cell.

Then the man in charge looked at me, probably seeing how skinny and scared I was, and said, "Take them off. He isn't going anywhere."

They took me outside, where there were even more goons with automatic weaponry, and loaded me into a Land Rover. As we drove through the city streets it soon become apparent that we were going to my home. For an all-too-brief moment I thought they were going to let me go. And then an indescribably worse thought struck me: "What are they planning to do with my family?"

When we arrived at my home two of the armed men went around to the back of the house while the rest escorted me to the front door. My mother was shocked to see me like that, and kept asking them what I had done wrong. They pushed past her without answering. She asked me, but even though I kept insisting I'd done nothing, I don't think she believed me.

The secret police invaded our home and began rummaging through everything. They didn't have a search warrant — in Iran in those days, the Savak didn't need one. They were effectively above the law. My mother, by now very frightened, tried to telephone my father, but the agents firmly prevented her. Meanwhile, they tore apart my room, confiscating books and papers.

I don't know if they found what they were looking for. After a while they stopped searching and led me back outside. They drove me back to the building where they had interrogated me. I was blindfolded and taken to the basement. They escorted me through a series of winding corridors — I remember counting my steps and noting whenever we turned left or right. It didn't help.

The guards removed my blindfold and locked me in a small, dark, barren cell. I couldn't see down the corridor, but I could hear terrible sounds, the screams and pleas of people being tortured not far away. Completely alone, helpless, still ignorant of why I had been arrested, I was more afraid than I had ever been, or ever have been since. I wondered whether I would be killed, or if I'd ever see my family and friends again, or if I'd ever see the sun or feel the wind on my face.

Like most teenagers, I had felt immortal and invincible. Now I saw just how quickly all the wonderful things we take for granted can be snatched away—no warning, no explanation, no safeguards. Huddled in that awful place, I determined that if I ever got out, I'd never take anything for granted ever again. I'd cherish every moment, make every action count. I would, as the poet says, "suck the marrow of life." If only I had another chance . . .

After three agonizing days I was released.

Only later did I learn how lucky I had been. As it turned out, my only "crime" had been to read the wrong books at the wrong time. Savak took a dim view of that, but not, thankfully, a dim enough view to have me executed or permanently imprisoned. I guess they figured I had learned my lesson.

And I did. But not, probably, the lesson they wanted to impart. Instead I learned the preciousness of life, of freedom, of the power of choice. I learned, during those dark and terrible days, to take control of my life.

I don't know how much more time is allotted to me. Every week, it seems, I hear about people my age dying in car accidents or fires, or from heart attacks or cancer, or getting shot or blown up. None of us know what's in store for us, so I'd advise only this: Be wise with time; respect it; never, ever waste it. Don't put off till tomorrow what you can do today — I know that sounds trite, but it's so very true.

Here's something I give all my students in my leadership seminars:

He was going to be all that he wanted to be — tomorrow.
None would be kinder or braver than he — tomorrow.
A friend who was troubled and weary he knew,

THE ONE PERCENT SOLUTION

Would be glad of a lift and needed it too,
On him he would call, see what he could do — tomorrow.
Each morning he'd stack up the letters he'd write —
tomorrow.
And thought of the folks he'd fill with delight — tomorrow.
The greatest of workers this man might have been,
The world would have opened its heart to him,
But in fact he passed and faded from view,
And all that was left when his living was through,
Was a mountain of things he intended to do — tomorrow.

Cindy Handy once told a story about a sullen, frequently depressed young man named Joe. Joe was never quite satisfied with his lot in life, and spent most of his time feeling sorry for himself. He wished he were richer, or taller, or better-looking, or smarter, or . . . well, you get the idea. In short, he spent a lot more time wishing than he did doing.

One day as Joe wandered along the town pier, he saw an old man fishing. The fish must've been biting that day, because the man already had a sizable haul, and Joe watched him reel in another good-sized specimen. Joe strolled over to watch, thinking that if only he had been lucky enough to bring in a catch like that, he could've sold the fish for some needed cash.

After a while, the old man turned to Joe and asked him to watch his line while he ran an errand or two. Joe gladly accepted. The fish kept biting, and Joe reeled them in. His self-pity quickly evaporated as he excitedly pulled in catch after catch.

When the old man returned, he insisted that Joe keep the fish he had caught, and as the boy happily bundled up his haul, said to him, "Young man, when you see other people getting what you want, don't waste time standing around and wishing — cast a line in for yourself."

Effective leaders know that success is rarely handed to them on the proverbial silver platter. Success requires hard work, active involvement, a willingness to learn. It also takes time. How we allocate our time determines not only our professional success, but very often our personal happiness. As I learned all those years ago, time is too precious a commodity to waste. "Never leave for tomorrow that which you can do today," said Benjamin Franklin.

In your business dealings, then, it's important for you to accord others the same respect for the value of their time that you'd want them to give you. Be punctual; don't skip appointments. Be as organized as possible to get the most out of your meetings. Be brief. "Brevity is pleasant," wrote Beltasar Gracian, "and it gets more done. In brief, good things may seem twice as good."

Eight Tips for Better Time Management

1. Spend time planning and organizing. Using your time to think and plan upcoming actions is time well spent. In fact, if you neglect to take the time to plan ahead, you are, by default, simply planning to fail. Organize your actions in a logical, sensible manner — the simplest approach is very often the best approach.

2. Prioritize. Use the 80-20 rule developed originally by the Italian economist Vilfredo Pareto. Pareto noted that 80 percent of the reward comes from just 20 percent of the effort. The key is being able to correctly identify which 20 percent is the crucial component for success. Once you've isolated it, you'll know exactly where you should be concentrating the bulk of your time and energy to maximize your return.

3. Use a to-do list. Write down your objectives, prioritize them, and then get busy accomplishing them. Weekly or even daily to-do lists are invaluable tools for helping you stick to a schedule — and it sure feels good to check off the tasks you've successfully completed. You might even care to create one that lists long-range personal and professional goals. Looking at it regularly will help keep you focused on your long-term ambitions: financial independence, physical fitness, promotion, etc. Feel free to continually reevaluate and re-prioritize any of your lists; there's no reason why they — and you — shouldn't be flexible when necessary.

4. Do the right thing. Noted management expert Peter Drucker says, "Doing the right thing is more important than doing things right." It's not as strange as it sounds. Doing the right thing is effectiveness; doing things right is efficiency.

Focus first on being an effective leader (identifying the right course of action), and only then on efficiency (doing it right). It's not, and shouldn't be, an either-or proposition — with practice you can be both an effective and astoundingly efficient leader. But since we're prioritizing, you'd be well advised to make sure you're choosing the correct thing to do right at the start. Remember that a wrong-headed action is no less wrong no matter how well you do it.

5. Avoid perfectionism. In an ideal world, everything you did would be perfect all the time. Unfortunately we live in a markedly less than ideal world, and a too-puritanical fixation on perfection can backfire, causing you needless delays, distress and discouragement. It can also sometimes be just another form of procrastination. So do the best you can whenever you can, but recognize your own fallibilities and make allowances.

6. Conquer procrastination. We all procrastinate, either because we're lazy, or the task ahead is a large or unpleasant one, or we're unsure of ourselves, or — that dreaded mantra — "we just don't feel like it." One way to combat it is Alan Lakein's "Swiss cheese" method. He advises that you break the task you're avoiding down into a handful of smaller, easily compartmentalized actions — sort of a miniature to-do list. Work on the smaller tasks one by one, finishing one before moving on to the next.

Alternately, you can set a timer and work on the overall task for some set period, say 15 minutes or half an hour. By starting little by little you'll be able to whittle the magnitude of the project down to a more manageable size.

7. Learn to say no. We talk a lot about not wanting to "spread ourselves too thin," but that's sometimes easier said than done. Too often we find ourselves unwilling to say no to additional responsibilities, duties and projects. But all that achieves is a further unnecessary diffusion of our limited energies, and help ensure that nothing we do is done to the best of our ability.

Don't muddy the waters. Be clear about what's important to you. Keep your energies directed squarely in those directions and don't hesitate to steer clear of the unimportant things in life. That's not avoiding responsibility — it's having the maturity to recognize your own limits, and the wisdom to know where your time is most profitably spent.

8. Reward yourself. Celebrate even small successes, personal and professional — it'll help keep you motivated and fulfilled. Take the time to smell the roses, to really enjoy the fruits of your labors. As Ann McGee-Cooper says, "If we learn to balance excellence in work with excellence in play, fun and relaxation, our lives become happier, healthier and a great deal more creative."

Conclusion

We can't know the future, so we should make the most out of the present. We must learn to respect time, to appreciate the moment at hand. As George Bernard Shaw said, "I want to be thoroughly used up when I die, for the harder I work the more I live. I rejoice in life for its own sake. Life is no 'brief candle' to me. It is a sort of splendid torch which I have got hold of for the moment, and I want to make it burn as brightly as possible before handing it on to future generations."

Effective leaders don't wait for good things to simply happen — they go out and make them happen. Adept time management techniques — advance planning, prioritizing, to-do lists, etc. — enable effective leaders to achieve the maximum results for their efforts.

THE ONE PERCENT SOLUTION

CH. 5 PERSONAL WORKSHEET

"Resolved — never to do anything which I should be afraid to do if it were the last hour of my life."

— Jonathan Edwards

I will improve my time-management skills by at least 1% in the following area:

_____

_____

_____

_____

I will benefit by this 1% improvement in the following way:

_____

_____

_____

_____

CHAPTER 6

Say the Right Thing

Tips for Effective Communication

"Communicating effectively enters into the results of every experience."

— Charles Wilkinson

Virginia was a woman who attended one of my leadership seminars a few years ago. She was a bright, articulate, thoroughly competent professional, the kind of employee a company feels lucky to have. But Virginia had one serious failing — she was absolutely terrified of getting up and speaking in front of a group of people.

She had always regarded her fear as an unfortunate and sometimes frustrating weakness, but not something that really detracted from her value as an employee or that might impede her chances for advancement within the company. Then along came an incident that forced her to change her mind and seek help in overcoming her phobia.

THE ONE PERCENT SOLUTION

Virginia had worked six months on a major project, the kind of thing that can make or break a career. And she did a bang-up job. But as the time to make the big presentation to management drew closer, Virginia found herself more and more afraid at the thought of having to stand up in front of all the corporate bigwigs and deliver her proposals. Finally she asked a co-worker, Frank, if he'd make the presentation in her place.

He did, and it was well-received by the corporate brass — so well-received, in fact, that Frank received a promotion shortly afterward. If only Virginia had had the self-confidence and communication know-how to get up and do it herself, the promotion likely would've been hers for the taking. Her insecurity about public speaking had become more than just a nuisance — it had cost her a valuable opportunity for career advancement.

Even if you've never had an experience like Virginia's, I'm willing to bet you've felt the public speaking jitters at least once in your life. I think all of us have experienced the sweaty palms, the butterflies in the stomach, the wobbly-kneed fear that we're going to make complete, utter fools of ourselves in front of a roomful of strangers. We may talk about "natural born speakers," but no one is genetically immune from stage fright; good speakers have simply conquered their nervousness through lots and lots of practice.

I remember a time, many years ago, when a group of us business owners were asked during a Chamber of Commerce meeting to stand up and say our names and the names of our respective companies. When my turn came, I could hear my heart thumping loud enough to be heard in the hall. But I took a deep breath, stood up shakily, and said . . . something. To this day I don't remember what it was, don't know if I even got my own name right.

But I survived. No one laughed, no one threw rotten vegetables at me, no one kicked me out into the street. And even if I didn't remember the particulars of what I said, I knew that I had said *something*. That was the important thing. I had faced my fear and was stronger for having done so. And the next time I stood up in front of a group of people to say a few words . . . well, I was still nervous, but it wasn't the same mind-numbing terror that I experienced that first time. And the time after that was better still. And the time after that . . .

If you've got chronic stage fright, what's worst thing you can do? Nothing. Fear feeds on fear. It's like the child who, convinced that there's a monster living in his closet, huddles in bed, terrified of making a sound, more sure with each passing minute that the monster is going to come out and eat him. And the longer he stays cowering under the covers the more afraid he becomes . . . until finally his parents come in, open the closet door and let him see for himself that there's nothing there, no monster, no reason to be afraid any more.

So if you're going to allay that fear of public speaking, to prove to yourself that it's nothing more substantial than the bogeyman (and trust me, it's not), you've got to take positive action. Instead of avoiding opportunities to speak, you've got to seek them out. Volunteer to give presentations at work, air your opinions at meetings, join speaking-oriented clubs like the Toastmasters. Take it slow and steady; concentrate on making that one percent change. It still won't be easy in the beginning — your nervousness won't magically disappear just because you want it to. But the more you speak the more at ease you'll be, and eventually you'll look back and wonder why you were ever afraid. Trust me, I know.

Kathlyn Gay hit the nail right on the head when she wrote, "Effective communication is the most important skill a person can have . . . in business, in the community and in the home."

There really *isn't* any characteristic more important. Think about it for a moment. No matter how solid your opinions may be, no matter how creative your solutions, no matter how discerning your perceptions, none of it really matters if you can't communicate those thoughts to others. Effective leaders must — *must*, absolutely and unequivocally — be able to communicate effectively. Without that ability, there's no way you can share your vision, your enthusiasm or your determination. Without communication, there's virtually no way to fashion the kind of teamwork so necessary in today's increasingly specialized workplace.

By learning how to communicate more confidently and creatively we're also really learning how to market our ideas more successfully. Our words, our body language and our tone all provide the "packaging" to catch the listener's interest and sell him or her on our suggestion. Poor presentation equals poor packaging, and that usually means no sale.

Consider generic food items. Their quality is about as good as their brand-name equivalents and their price significantly less. There's no question that from a purely economic standpoint they're a real bargain. So why don't more people fill their shopping carts with generics?

Simple. Packaging. Brand-name products come in colorful, eye-catching containers and have ear-catching, memorable names. They seem to be inviting us to buy them, telling us that they're unique, special, better. Generic items, by comparison, just seem so *dull*. We know they're the better deal, but there's no glamour there. Instead of leaping out to grab our attention, they seem content to silently sit on the shelf until their expiration dates.

Effective communication, whether in public speaking or one-on-one conversation, is our means of advertising the merits of our ideas. We can't simply depend on our audience to discover those merits on their own — we've got to actively call attention to them.

Let's talk about some specifics. Every time we speak we should have a definite purpose (besides hearing our own gums flap, that is):

1. To entertain.
2. To inform.
3. To convince.
4. To prompt others to take action.

As leaders we're mostly called upon to inspire others to

take action. That doesn't mean, however, that you shouldn't strive to be entertaining, informative or convincing. But before ever opening your mouth during a meeting or standing up before an audience, or even making a phone call, be sure you know exactly what your purpose is in doing so. And before you say anything, make sure that you first *have* something to say.

And after you've spoken, reflect for a minute or two on what you *wanted* to say, what you *think* you said, and what you *actually* said. The discrepancies may surprise you — sometimes we get so flustered at having to speak publicly that we say something very different from what was intended. That's OK — don't retreat back into your shell of silence. As you become more comfortable and confident thanks to practice, the gaps between intent, perception and reality will narrow significantly. Remember what I said earlier about there being no "born speakers," just more experienced speakers.

When addressing a group, it always helps to have a formula you can structure your address on. A very simple but nonetheless effective formula is the EAR sequence.

E stands for a specific EVENT or EXPERIENCE you use as the foundation of your presentation. It should illustrate the point you want to make to your listeners, and be engaging enough that it captures their attention. Remember to mention (when appropriate) when it happened, where it happened, who was involved, and what actually transpired. Use action words and dialogue to energize the account.

A stands for the specific ACTION you want your listeners to take. Use active verbs and be brief — get right to the point.

R stands for REWARD. Here you want to let your listeners see the positive benefits of taking the action you just proposed. Be as specific as possible — try to personalize your reward message to match your audience's goals, interests and expectations.

Used correctly — and again, with practice — the EAR method will reap results. Learn to fine-tune it to suit different audiences and different situations and you'll be well on your way to being a concise, informative and persuasive speaker.

Kathlyn Gay isolated four areas crucial to effective communication: word choice, body language, listening habits and responses. Each of these is a skill, and as such, can be developed with effort and practice. In the next few pages we'll take a closer look at each of them.

Word Choice

One of the best examples of the effectiveness of creative word choice is a story a former student of mine, a woman named Vicki, related to the class one day. It seems that the family dog, much to the family's surprise and dismay, unexpectedly gave birth to a litter of 10 puppies. As the pups neared the end of the weaning period, Vicki and her husband put an ad in the local paper: FREE TO GOOD HOME — 10 ADORABLE PUPPIES. Response to the ad was meager, however, and after two weeks the family still had seven puppies left.

So they altered their tactics. They changed the newspaper ad to read: FREE TO GOOD HOME — 1 UGLY AND 6 PRETTY PUPPIES. No sooner had the ad appeared than the phone calls started — all from people eager to know if the family still had the "ugly" one. By the next evening they had given away the "ugly" puppy seven times!

In choosing the right words, put yourself in your audience's position — what would *you* want to hear? What words would be most effective in persuading *you*? Now try to craft your word choices to appeal specifically to your audience — to their likes, dislikes, moods, backgrounds, personalities, etc. The more in tune you are with your listeners, the better the odds that your words will strike a responsive chord within them.

Winston Churchill is a terrific example of a speaker who understood the supreme importance of words. His undisputed mastery of the English language did not come easily, however — it was the result of years of diligent practice. As a young man he seemed an unlikely orator — short, slightly hunched, physically unprepossessing. His voice was unattractive, and he suffered from a speech impediment that was part lisp and part stammer. Early in his career one observer called him a "medium-sized, undistinguished young man, with an unfortunate lisp in his voice . . . and he lacks face."

SAY THE RIGHT THING

Churchill overcame his oratorical shortcomings through, in his own words, "hard, hard work." He studied and memorized the speeches of famous orators and spent hours in front of his mirror practicing his delivery, body language and facial expressions.

And, perhaps more significantly, he carefully crafted his speeches, editing, refining, pruning phrases or words that weren't quite right, painstakingly searching for those that were. The process wasn't quick and it wasn't easy — there were no gimmicks. But, in the end, his speeches were as perfect as he could make them, and it's been said that although not all his speeches were successful, very few were slovenly.

And because of Churchill's intense attention to detail, he gave us some of the most stirring speeches of this or any other age, capturing perfectly in words the emotions of his listeners:

"The whole fury and might of the enemy must very soon be turned on us. Hitler knows that he will have to break us in this island or lose the war. If we can stand up to him, all Europe may be free and the life of the world may move forward into broad, sunlit uplands. But if we fail, then the whole world, including the United States, including all that we have known and cared for, will sink into the abyss of a new Dark Age made more sinister, and perhaps more protracted, by the lights of perverted science. Let us therefore brace ourselves to our duties and so bear ourselves that if the British Empire and its Commonwealth last for a thousand years, men will still say, 'This was their finest hour.' "

Whew.

Body Language

As important as it is for you as a speaker to employ the right words, it's no less necessary for you to use the appropriate body language. Too often we're unaware of these physical messages we're sending our audience, but studies have shown that they're of crucial significance in both holding listeners' attention and actually winning them over. Nonverbal signals convey your enthusiasm, your confidence, your professional competence and, certainly not least, your sincerity. No matter how eloquent your words are, if they're not supported by the right body language they're likely to be unconvincing.

Edwin Dobbs related an occasion where a little bit of luck and a lot of pluck led to stardom for one young man.

One summer day in 1974, 11-year-old Stanley Burrell set his cassette player on the blacktop outside the Oakland Coliseum. Loud, raucous music boomed from the tiny speaker, and then, even more incongruously, Stanley began to dance, first spinning on his toes, then shuffling rhythmically side to side, then falling into a deep leg split.

Oakland A's fans who had come to see their team play the White Sox stopped to watch, erupting into whistles and applause when Stanley brought his routine to a close. He nimbly bounced up and passed through the crowd collecting change in an upturned baseball cap. Then he spotted Charles O. Finley, the Athletics' outspoken owner. Stanley was no born speaker, but he was already a consummate performer and he recognized the opportunity Finley represented.

"Hey, Mr. Finley! Mr. Finley!" he yelled. "Can I go inside and watch the game?"

For a second the two stared at each other, the streetwise kid trying to cadge a free pass and the rough-n-ready Chicago mill worker who had made a fortune selling insurance before building a major league empire. Most people, much less most 11-year-olds, would have been too intimidated to look a man like Finley right in the eye. Not Stanley. He met Finley's gaze with an impudent smile.

And maybe since Finley was, in his own way, as much of a showman as young Stanley, he appreciated the boy's gumption. "Come on," he grumbled, turning towards the gate. Stanley and his friends watched the game from Finley's personal box, a privilege usually reserved for a rich and favored few.

During the game, Finley turned to Stanley and his friends and asked, "So what do you think of my team's chances this year?"

Stanley's friends were too flustered to do much more than smile and stammer, but not Stanley. "The A's are good," he said confidently, "but not as good as they will be in a few years when I'm down there hitting home runs for them."

Finley chuckled. His boyhood dream had been to be a ballplayer, too. In Stanley he saw a little bit of himself. "Kid, you want a job?" he asked.

Neither Finlay nor Stanley could have appreciated the fatefulness of the moment. Stanley's parents had divorced years before, and his mother struggled to keep her five children fed, clothed and schooled. She encouraged them to avoid the pitfalls that trapped so many ghetto kids, to work hard, to stay out of trouble and to take advantage of opportunity when it presented itself. Stanley's dance moves and, just as importantly, his self-assurance and confidence, had provided him with just such an opportunity and true to his mother's advice he wasted no time in grabbing hold of it.

Stanley became Finley's personal gofer during games, ferrying team announcements from the front office to the press box and Finley's messages to the dugout. He earned $5 per game. The players soon took a liking to the brash young man, even inviting him onto the field during batting practice. One day Reggie Jackson said to him, "You know who you look like? You're the spittin' image of Hammerin' Hank. Guess that makes you Little Hammer." The nickname stuck.

Stanley finished high school and attended community college. He didn't make the baseball team, but he did devote himself to his music, writing rap songs and gospel tunes. He signed himself simply "Hammer." Despite disappointments, he never stopped believing in himself and in his ability. His perseverance paid off in 1988 when a representative of Capitol Records saw his act at a local club and signed the 25-year-old to a record deal — with a $600,000 advance.

The kind of enthusiasm, sincerity and confidence that

young Stanley Burrell displayed breeds opportunity. Consider the story of Dizzy Dean.

Dizzy so loved the game of baseball that even after his playing days were over he wanted to be a part of the Big Show. He thought he might try his hand at radio broadcasting, but his folksy, ungrammatical delivery and lack of any formal training seemed formidable obstacles. Nevertheless, he felt sure that his knowledge of the game and his enthusiasm for it would make him an effective communicator, and that confidence won over the radio executives, who decided to take a chance on him. They weren't wrong, either — Dizzy consistently drew a large listening audience, for whom his lack of polish was overshadowed by his extensive knowledge and intense pleasure in the game.

Listening Habits

Communication is a two-way street. For it to be effective, someone has to be listening. If everyone is talking, all we have is noise. So it's imperative to remember that our listening skills are as important as our speaking skills. Clear communication is about avoiding confusion — eschew obfuscation! — and cutting to the heart of the matter. That involves sincere dialogue. And dialogue implies listening.

Unless we listen, really listen, to what the other person is saying, we can't honestly expect them to listen carefully to us. Everyone, no matter who they are, would rather have the undivided attention of their audience than the sinking feeling that they're simply providing the background noise for someone's daydreams. No one likes being ignored. On the other hand, as Dale Carnegie said, "You could make more friends in two months by becoming interested in other people than you can in two years by trying to get other people interested in you." By simply listening attentively to others, you've already gone a long way towards winning them over.

And sometimes, you know, you might even learn a thing or two by listening to someone else. It might be a facet of a problem you hadn't considered, or a solution that's better suited to the situation at hand or a viewpoint that's as valid as yours. By listening with an open mind (and that's important to stress here) you might avoid any number of unnecessary and unpleasant disagreements — maybe you and your counterpart are closer on an issue than you thought. You'll never find out, though, unless you shut your mouth and open your ears.

Jennifer Hilton told a story about her father's days as a student at Mississippi State University back in the 60s. Her grandfather hadn't had the opportunity to attend college and was determined that his son would get a degree.

At the end of a frustrating first term, after spending all night studying for a chemistry test, Jennifer's dad came the conclusion that he'd never use all this academic stuff in the real world and that he was wasting his time. He called his father and said, "Pop, I'm leaving college."

His father, a man of few words but great wisdom, didn't raise his voice, didn't become angry, didn't forbid his son to do so. He simply said, a little casually even, "Really, son? Where in the world are you going?"

The son thought for a moment and hung up — and went back to studying. He had listened well to what was said and what was implied by his father's words.

Responses

A few years ago I sold my car. I took the payment check to my bank to deposit it, and after standing in line for what seemed an interminable amount of time, I found myself at the teller's window facing a clearly agitated young woman. It was apparent that she wasn't having a good day. Curtly she took the check, examined it, and walked over to speak to another employee. I waited patiently — at first. But she didn't come back to her counter, and I could see her moving around back there, talking to several other people. I felt ignored, and wondered if she'd forgotten about me — or if there was something wrong.

My frustration mounted, and I felt like snapping at her when — if — she ever returned. But fortunately I got a grip on my negative emotions. "C'mon, I teach this stuff," I reminded myself, taking a couple of deep breaths.

And when she finally came back to me, I looked at her name tag, smiled, and said as personably as I could, "Debbie, I hope everything is all right?"

It was like the clouds had parted and the sun shone through. She immediately smiled back, clearly surprised and relieved that I hadn't lashed out at her. She assured me that everything was fine, that she and the others had simply wanted to verify as thoroughly as possible that the check was good. I thanked her for her care and effort.

If I hadn't taken the time to think about my response, if I had succumbed to my knee-jerk reaction to castigate her for her poor customer-relation skills, I would have been doing both of us a disservice. Thankfully I was able to choke down my frustration and respond positively and constructively. But how many times do we allow negative tension to dictate the outcome? How many times do we simply lash out at another? And how many times do we regret doing so? Temper tantrums, biting sarcasm and insults rarely facilitate effective communication. Think before you speak — especially when you're angry.

My experience with Debbie the bank-teller also illustrates a few tips that tend to increase your audience's receptivity and avoid communication faux-pas:

1. We all love to hear the sound of our own name. It makes us feel like we're the center of the speaker's attention. It makes us feel special and unique, and helps make any encounter more personal and sincere. But how often do you call someone by name, even when they're wearing a name tag? Try it sometime and see how they perk up. I think you'll be pleasantly surprised.

2. Negative assumptions create negative reactions.
Likewise, positive assumptions can produce positive results
for all involved. As long as I held on to my negative assumptions — that I was being ignored or that something had gone
wrong — I was primed to respond negatively with anger and
anxiety. When I discarded those assumptions the situation
immediately became less tense.

When I was a boy, I was filled with a great deal of anger.
I was constantly in fights, and although my parents tried
everything, nothing seemed to soothe me. They kept trying,
though. Finally they hit on a novel solution. I remember one
day when my mother and grandmother talked, just talked,
with me. We talked for hours, until long after dark, and at
the end of it I realized that something wonderful had happened — all that internal rage had subsided, like a fire being slowly extinguished.

I saw things from a different vantage point — my negative assumptions had been replaced with more positive ones.
And that made all the difference.

**3. We should make it a point to offer sincere appre-
ciation for others' actions.** It doesn't cost anything to com-
pliment someone else, but some people are still remarkably
stingy about doing so. That's a mistake. We all like to feel
appreciated, and we tend to go the extra mile for those people
who make us feel that way. It's a win-win situation. I remember once reading, "If at the end of the day you feel dog-
tired, maybe it's because you growled all day."

135

I ask all my leadership classes: "Is there anyone here who gets all the appreciation they deserve?" And you know what? Out of the thousands of people I've asked, not one — *not one* — has ever said yes. I guess we could all do with a little more appreciation in our lives.

Conclusion

Effective communication is nothing more and nothing less than a learned skill. With practice anyone can become a better, more confident speaker. Remember to choose your words carefully, to demonstrate your enthusiasm both verbally and non-verbally, to genuinely listen to others, and to think about what you want to say before you say it. Be clear and concise, always try to illustrate your points, and include a potential benefit for the audience if they follow your suggestions. Focus on the little things — you'll be surprised at the difference they make.

CH. 6 PERSONAL WORKSHEET

"The difference between the almost-right word and the right word is really a large matter — 'tis the difference between the lightning-bug and the lightning."

— Mark Twain

I will better my communication skills by at least 1% by focusing on this one area:

_____

_____

_____

_____

I will benefit by this 1% improvement in the following way:

_____

_____

_____

_____

CHAPTER 7

Final Thoughts

Continuing the Journey

"The mode in which the inevitable comes to pass is through effort."

— Oliver Wendell Holmes

We've talked a great deal in the preceding pages about what leadership is. So now I'd like to mention a few things that leadership *isn't*.

• **Leadership is not a position.** Almost anyone can be elected, selected, anointed, appointed or promoted to a position of leadership. But that position in and of itself doesn't make a leader. For people to respect you as a leader, you have to demonstrate the skills we've already talked about — enthusiasm, effective communication skills (including listening), good time management and goal-setting/problem-solving abilities, persistence and confidence. Getting paid to be a leader doesn't automatically make you one.

• **Leadership is not a 100-yard dash.** Effective leaders train for a marathon. They know that becoming a great leader takes time, effort and dedication. It can't happen in a weekend. In the final analysis, leadership is really sort of a long distance relay race, with the baton passing from generation to generation.

• **Leadership is not always being in the spotlight.** Sometimes behind-the-scenes leadership is even more effective. You don't have to be the boss to be a leader — everyone, no matter their rank, position or salary, can be a leader.

• **Leadership isn't about making more money.** Granted, more money is always nice, but it's a poor primary goal for a leader. Good leaders are motivated by a desire to improve themselves and others as individuals, by a desire to better the world around them, by a desire to make a positive difference in people's lives.

• **Leadership isn't egotism.** Confidence is a tremendous asset, but arrogance is one of those traits that can poison the well. No one appreciates smugness. Determination is admirable; stubbornness is not. Know your abilities — and equally, know your limitations. That'll help keep you appropriately humble.

FINAL THOUGHTS

• **Leadership doesn't exist in a vacuum.** Leaders can't go it alone. They depend upon the support of those around them, and if they lose that support, they cease to be effective leaders.

• **Leadership is not being indecisive.** Think through your decisions; prepare as thoroughly as you can by gathering knowledge and weighing your options. But when the time comes to act — act!

• **Leadership is not about blaming others.** Leadership is first and foremost about personal responsibility. Don't try to duck that fact. Success or failure, the buck stops with you.

I want to encourage all of you to take what you've learned in these chapters and apply them — and keep applying them. Effective leaders have made a habit of effective leadership skills. Don't underestimate the power of habit — it can be a tremendous asset if used correctly. Here's something I share with my students in my leadership seminars:

You may know me.
I'm your constant companion.
I'm your greatest helper;
I'm your heaviest burden.
I will push you onward or drag you down to failure.
I am at your command.

THE ONE PERCENT SOLUTION

Half the tasks you do might as well be turned over to me.
I'm able to do them quickly,
And I'm able to do them the same every time if that's what
   you want.

I'm easily managed — all you've got to do is be firm with
   me.
Show me exactly how you want it done.
After a few lessons I'll do it automatically.

I am the servant of all great men and women;
Of course, servant of the failures as well.
I've made all the great individuals who have ever been
   great,
And I've made the failures, too.

But I work with the precision of a marvelous computer,
With the intelligence of a human being.
You may run me for profit, or you may run me to ruin;
It makes no difference to me.

Take me. Be easy with me and I will destroy you.
Be firm with me and I'll put the world at your feet.
Who am I?
I am habit.

We are all creatures of habit. We simply have to make a
choice about what habits will govern our lives. Great habits

make great leaders; bad habits create failures.

To form good habits, our learning process must pass through three levels. Keep that in mind as you reflect on the lessons of this book.

1. Experience. The experience itself can come in many forms and impact us on many levels.

2. Identification. What's the significance of that experience?

3. Generalization. What's the future value of the experience and what lessons can we draw from it?

Thanks for taking the time to read this book. I hope it was and will be profitable to you. If you have any success stories or illustrative anecdotes you'd like to share, by all means send them to me, Bijan Afkami, in care of Bijan International, 11776 Jollyville Road, Suite 250, Austin, Texas 78759. I'd love to hear from you.

I'd like to leave you with one final story:

There was once a young man who, as callow young men are apt to do, believed he had life all figured out. He approached the wise old village elder one day. In his cupped, closed hands he held a bird, hidden from view. He held out his hands to the elder and said, "Old man, in my hands I hold a bird. Tell me, since you're supposed to be so wise: is it alive or is it dead?"

THE ONE PERCENT SOLUTION

The old man knew that it was a trick. If he said the bird was dead, the young man would open his hands and let it fly away. If he said it was alive, the young man would instantly crush the bird.

So instead he answered, "Young man, you alone can determine that. It's all in your hands."

No matter what you choose to do or where you choose to go, remember that one vital lesson: it's all in your hands!

FINAL THOUGHTS

RECOMMENDED READING

The number of leadership books in existence is truly staggering. Here's a sampling of some of those which have given me guidance, inspiration and knowledge over the years:

Alexander, Scott. *Rhinoceros Success.*

Anthony, Robert. *The Ultimate Secrets of Total Self-Confidence.*

Ash, Mary Kay. *Mary Kay on People Management.*

Blanchard, Kenneth and Spencer Johnson. *The One Minute Manager.*

Bradford, David and Allan R. Cohen. *Managing for Excellence.*

Brown, Les. *Live Your Dreams.*

Brown, W. Steven. *13 Fatal Errors Managers Make.*

Buck, Lee. *Tapping Your Secret Source of Power.*

Carnegie, Dale and Associates. *Managing Through People.*

Carnegie, Dale. *How to Stop Worrying and Start Living.*

Carnegie, Dale. *How to Win Friends and Influence People.*

Conwell, Russell. *Acres of Diamonds.*

Cooper, Kenneth, M.D. *The Aerobics Program for Total Well-Being.*

Danzig, Robert. *The Leader Within You.*

DeBruyn, Robert I. *Causing Others to Want Your Leadership.*

Dobson, James. *What Wives Wish Their Husbands Knew*

THE ONE PERCENT SOLUTION

About Women.

Dyer, Wayne W. *You'll See It When You Believe It.*

Follett, Ken. *On Wings of Eagles.*

Glass, Kinder and Ward. *Positive Power for Successful Salesmen.*

Graham, Stedman. *You Can Make It Happen.*

Gschwandtner, Gerhard. *Superachievers.*

Hayes, Ira. *Yak! Yak! Yak!*

Hersey, Paul and Kenneth Blanchard. *Management of Organizational Behavior.*

Hickman, Craig and Michael Silva. *Creating Excellence.*

Hill, Napoleon. *Success Through a Positive Mental Attitude.*

Hunsaker, Phillip L. and Anthony J. Alessandra. *The Art of Managing People.*

Jones, Charlie. *Life Is Tremendous.*

Maltz, Maxwell. *Psycho-cybernetics.*

Mandino, Og. *The Greatest Miracle in the World.*

Marshall, Peter and David Manuel. *The Light and the Glory.*

Peale, Norman Vincent. *The Power of Positive Thinking.*

Robbins, Anthony. *Awaken the Giant Within.*

Robbins, Anthony. *Unlimited Power.*

Schuller, Robert H. *Tough Times Don't Last, but Tough People Do.*

Schwartz, David J. *The Magic of Thinking Big.*

Smith, Fred. *You and Your Network.*

Spickard, Anderson and Barbara R. Thompson. *Dying for a Drink.*

Teaff, Grant. *I Believe.*

RECOMMENDED READING

Waitley, Denis. *Seeds of Greatness.*

Ziglar, Zig. *Raising Positive Kids in a Negative World.*

Ziglar, Zig. *See You at the Top.*

ABOUT THE AUTHOR

Bijan Afkami is the president of Bijan International.

Born and raised in Iran, he came to the United States in 1977 to pursue the American Dream. As a junior in college, Bijan financed the purchase of a pizza restaurant where he had worked as a delivery driver by assuming debts owed to creditors, suppliers and the government. The following year he increased business 700% while completing his degree. By the age of 27, Bijan had become a millionaire with several successful businesses and substantial real estate holdings.

As a result of the downturn of the Austin real estate market in the late 80s, Bijan was forced into bankruptcy and the foreclosure of his home. With barely enough money for a deposit on a new rental home, he began again on the road to personal and financial success.

Bijan attributes his success to the lessons he learned through overcoming adversity and to his ability to work with others. He has spent years researching and developing programs that teach people how to increase their effectiveness in achieving their goals. Bijan International programs have enhanced the productivity of many organizations, from Fortune 500 companies to sole proprietorships.

In 1993, Motorola, Inc. retained the services of Bijan International and to date more than 2000 Motorola employees have completed the training. The same program, moreover, has been successfully utilized by correctional institutions in the state of Texas.

 # Leadership Program

Bijan International's Leadership Program has been successfully implemented by both large and small companies, from Fortune 500 giants to sole proprietorships. Motorola, Inc. has made extensive use of it — over 2000 Motorola employees have graduated from the program to date.

- **9 weekly sessions**
- **Full class participation — no lectures**
- **Practical class application of leadership principles**
- **Continuous positive feedback encourages participants to expand their individual comfort zones**
- **Spirited coaching and support**

The Leadership Program succeeds largely because of the mutual commitment that exists between Bijan International and the course participants. If you are committed to improving any of the areas listed below in your personal or professional life, Bijan International is committed to helping you attain your goals.

If you would like to know more about Bijan International's Leadership Program, call 1-888-550-LEAD for a free brochure or write to Bijan International, 11776 Jollyville Road, Suite 250, Austin, TX 78759.

CALL TOLL FREE TODAY! 1-888-550-LEAD

 # Executive Coaching

Executive Coaching is a highly personalized career and performance learning process. Coaching leads executives through a tailored process in which they develop a clear understanding of the skills and behaviors required to achieve personal and organizational success. Although each experience is different, all our coaching projects include:

- **Initial exploration of consulting relationship**
- **Establishing objectives and desired outcomes**
- **Formulating an individual diagnostic plan**
- **Establishing goals and a plan of action**
- **Taking action and cycling feedback**
- **Establishing a foundation for continuous growth and development**

As organizations change to meet the needs of a global economy in the complex information age, they need a workforce that can rise to meet new demands. Executive Coaching may be the key they need..

If you would like to know more about Bijan International's Executive Coaching, call 1-888-550-LEAD for a free brochure or write to Bijan International, 11776 Jollyville Road, Suite 250, Austin, TX 78759.

THE ONE PERCENT SOLUTION

Leadership Through Action

by **Bijan Afkami**

- -